MESSIAH AND THE TABERNACLE

Exodus 25 – 30

A 16-Part Bible Study

Study Manuscripts
Available from
HaDavar Messianic Ministries

Anti-Missionary Arguments

Comfort During Difficult Times

Biblical Perspectives on the Middle East

And I Will Bless You:

Studies in the Abrahamic Covenant

MESSIAH
and the Tabernacle

EXODUS 25-30

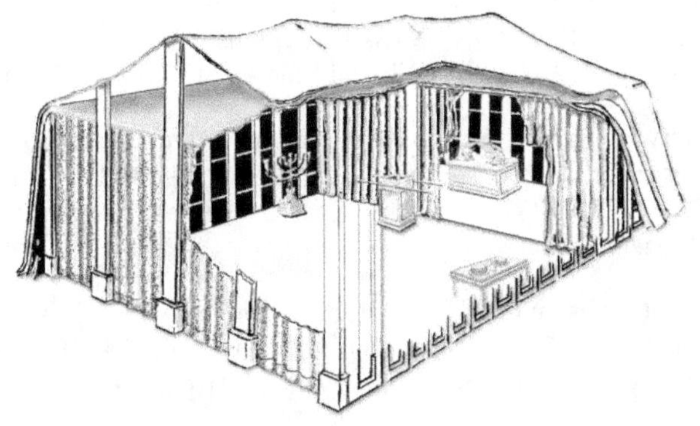

A 16-PART BIBLE STUDY

by ROBERT MORRIS, M.Div.

We are not to be walking
Bible encyclopedias
but to move beyond that point
and live out what we are learning
"in the trenches"!

The result is spiritual maturity.

Robert Morris

✿ ✿ ✿

The Author on the Question:

Why study scripture from the Jewish perspective?

We will get a more accurate understanding of the truth God was trying to communicate if we look at it through the eyes of the person to whom it was given. When we read the Bible through those eyes, through that grid, through those filters, we will get a clearer understanding of what God meant. That is the importance of taking a look at the **historical significance**.

We will also look at the **Messianic significance** and will see how the scriptures as a whole proclaim Jesus as the Messiah.

The final step will be to make an **application** from what we have learned. We will try to apply each section of scripture to our lives today.

✿ ✿ ✿

Dedication

To the team, for the glory of God

Debbie Morales, Susan Morris,
Beverly Smith, Joni Prinjinski

Acknowledgements

Thirty years ago, I began a career in Jewish outreach as a volunteer with Ariel Ministries. Twenty years ago, after completing seminary training, I was asked to teach a one-week course on the subject "Messiah and the Tabernacle" at Ariel's adult Bible camp, Camp Shoshanah. The course was not part of the established five-year program of studies at the camp, rather it was a test course to evaluate my teaching skills and approach. I guess I passed the test because I was asked to teach courses that were part of the established program for the next nine years.

Toward the end of that period of time, I left Ariel Ministries to become the Director and primary teacher of HaDavar Messianic Ministries in Orange County California. I felt led of the Lord to start a school of biblical and Jewish studies in order to increase the effectiveness and scope of Jewish outreach in Orange County. The first class I offered, again as a test, to see if the idea and unique format of the school would be received, was "Messiah and the Tabernacle." The class and format were well received and the HaDavar School of Biblical and Jewish Studies has been offering classes for about ten years at this time.

That original class was recorded and Debbie Vaughn (now Morales), one of the students, volunteered to type up the tape recording. She did a great job turning the tape into a raw, unformatted, electronic file. After that the file languished for a number of years until we decided to publish it as a manuscript through HaDavar. Then my wife, Susan, turned Debbie's electronic file into a marketable, properly-formatted manuscript.

Eventually, we decided to see if we could publish our first formal book. At that time, Beverly Smith, a HaDavar student and accomplished Christian author (pen name Beverly Bush), volunteered to give the existing manuscript an edit. Her expertise and encouragement moved the manuscript another step closer to publication. To my sorrow, Beverly has since gone to be with the Lord.

Now, under the capable hands of my publisher Joni Prinjinski, this class which started out 20 years ago will become my first book, just as it was my first study. The label, Purple Raiment, is the educational Messianic Jewish imprint of JHousePublishing. To summarize the history of this material, it was my first Ariel Ministries class, my first HaDavar School of Biblical and Jewish Studies class, and now my first book. I am grateful to the Lord that Joni feels it will be a valuable contribution to her Messianic series.

I want to thank our Lord and Messiah, Yeshua, for His guidance and direction in bringing this book to fruition. It is my desire that the teaching of the Word of God in this form will be used of the Lord to draw the reader, whether believing or seeking, to Himself.

- Pastor Robert Morris

CONTENTS

CONTENTS

TABLE OF FIGURES

1. INTRODUCTION AND OVERVIEW

INTRODUCTION

HaDavar Messianic Ministries welcomes you to our study of Messiah and the Tabernacle. Relatively few Bible studies focus on the construction and descriptions of the Tabernacle in the latter half of Exodus. Yet key scriptures from the book of Exodus provide a treasure chest of revelation about both the construction and the significance of Israel's Tabernacle.

HaDavar approaches the Bible with a two-fold philosophy to take you, the reader, to a richer understanding of scripture. The first principle is that a serious, in-depth study of the Bible should not be dry or strictly academic in nature. Rather, it should be relevant. It should be meaningful, challenging, and inspiring to the believer who loves to dig deeply into the scripture for its treasures. The second is that a study of the Bible should not be shallow, based on poor and deficient exegesis. It should not be focused strictly on the emotions and emphasize making us feel good at the expense of biblical quality and accurate understanding.

HaDavar wants to reach a balance between two extremes. We want God to speak to your hearts as well as your heads as you read and study His word. We want to offer you a reliable explanation of scripture and an accurate understanding of the text. At the same time, we want to make the Bible come alive in relevance and meaning for daily life.

HaDavar, which in Hebrew means "The Word," presents the scriptures from a Jewish perspective. Jewish culture and Jewish thinking is the foundation of biblical thought not only found during the time of the Ancient Near East when the Old Testament was written, but also during the first century when the New Testament was written.

Understanding the Word of God in the context of its Jewish background changes the student's comprehension suddenly from black and white to living color. Simply put, the Bible and its timeless truths come to life.

OVERVIEW

What is the Tabernacle? The Tabernacle is a worship structure that God commanded Israel to make. This worship structure is described in chapters 25-30 of the book of Exodus. Those are the chapters we will be looking at closely in this study.

If you had visited the nation of Israel during its infancy, you would have noted how prominent the Tabernacle was. It sat on a plot of ground in the midst of the camp of Israel, which was surrounded by the adjacent nations of the world (see Figure 1). On this plot of ground, the Tabernacle was bounded by an outer court enclosed by a linen fence about 150 feet long and 75 feet wide (see Figure 2). The layout was oriented in an east/west direction with the entrance at the eastern end.

Figure 1. Concept of the Tabernacle

Let us take a quick tour of the Tabernacle. We'll start at the entrance to the outer court at the linen fence on the east side of the Tabernacle court. The left side of the drawing above is the eastern side of the Tabernacle court. It is important to note that only Jewish people would be allowed beyond the fence into the Tabernacle compound itself. If you were a gentile (non-Jewish), you would not be allowed inside the compound. If you were Jewish, man or woman, you could move through the entrance, and as you did, the very first thing you would encounter would be a large altar made of bronze. As you continued walking, you would pass the altar, and soon you would stand beside a large basin of water. Another few steps and now you would be standing at the entrance to a rather large tent approximately 45 feet long, 15 feet wide, and 15 feet high.

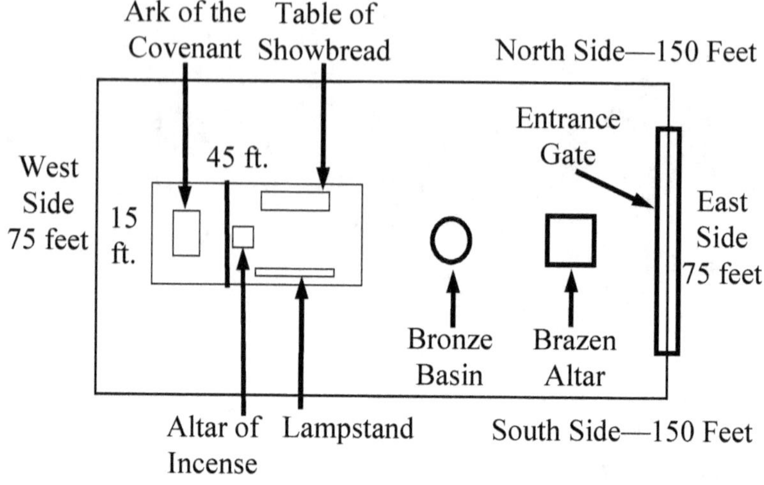

Figure 2. The Tabernacle Compound

If you were just a common person in the nation of Israel, you could go no further than outside the entrance to the tent. But if you were a Levite—that is, a member of the priestly tribe—you could enter into this very large tent. You'd step into a magnificent front room called the Holy Place. You would find yourself surrounded by golden frames, by stunning embroidered wall hangings, and by three pieces of golden furniture. On your right would sit a small table containing two stacks of unleavened bread. In front of you at the far end of the room would sit a small incense altar. On your left, the room would be illuminated by the light of a solid gold menorah or lamp stand.

As a Levite standing inside the tent, you would notice a curtain in front of you at the far end of the room, approximately 30 feet from the entrance. This curtain (or veil) would screen the front room in which you are standing from a smaller room at the rear of the tent. The small room was called the Holy of Holies or the Most Holy

Place. Yet even if you were a Levite, the Holy Place is as far as you could go.

However, if you were the High Priest, you would be allowed beyond that curtain or veil into the Most Holy Place, into the Holy of Holies. Upon entering the Holy of Holies, you would discover a cubical room, 15 feet by 15 feet by 15 feet, containing only one small, but highly significant, golden box. This box is called the Ark of the Covenant. The room itself would not have any kind of lamp stand or source of illumination, but it would be illuminated nonetheless. Standing there, you would see that the room was dominated by an unearthly glow. Just above this box, you would stand face-to-face with the very glory of God. The glory of God would illuminate the Most Holy Place. On this very brief tour, you have just experienced the awe-inspiring Tabernacle of Israel.

Significance of the Tabernacle

A question now presents itself: *What is the significance of all these things? What is the meaning of the courtyard and the altar and the basin, the tent, the front room, the rear room, and the glory of God?* These are the questions we will attempt to answer as we go through this study.

We all instinctively know that there is more to the Tabernacle than its outward appearance, its floor plan, and the fact that it is 150 feet long by 75 feet wide. The Tabernacle is highly symbolic, rich with spiritual truth.

We are not alone in our quest. The mystery of the Tabernacle has been obvious for many generations. We read these comments in chapter 7 from the *Hertz Pentateuch,* a Jewish study Bible written by Rabbi Dr. J. H. Hertz:

> Practically all commentators are agreed that the sanctuary was a symbol and its purpose was to impress the children of man with spiritual teachings. What, however, were the spiritual teachings which the tabernacle symbolized? This question offered full scope to the ingenuity of mystic interpreters, ancient and modern, Jewish and non-Jewish, who declared the sanctuary to be an epitome of that which is presented on a larger scale in the universe as a whole and an emblem of religions [sic] profoundest teachings on life and eternity.[1]

We see a number of key words and phrases in Rabbi Hertz's comments such as "symbol," "emblem," and "the epitome of that which is presented in the universe as a whole."

In an article in *The Jewish Encyclopedia* on the Tabernacle, the writer makes similar comments:

> It is probable that the characteristic features of the place of worship in the Old Testament bore, in addition to their outward appearance, their outward purpose, an inner relationship to religious ideas.[2]

In other words, there is more to the Tabernacle than the outward appearance.

Finally, here is a quote from an article in the *Jerusalem Post* dated February 20, 1997. Written by Pinchas Giller, it is entitled "The Sign Post to Paradox. Does Judaism require a Holy Place?" Giller makes a similar observation:

---

[1] Dr. J. H. Hertz, *The Pentateuch and Haftorahs*, (London, England: Soncino Press) 1987, 325.

[2] Jewish Encyclopedia.com: "Tabernacle," *www.jewishencyclopedia.com/ view.jsp?artid=3&letter=T&search=tabernacle*

The dimension, declarations, and rituals of the tabernacle take up the better part of the books of Exodus and Leviticus and make up a large part of the content of the Torah. Comprising such a large part of the law of content, these texts demand serious theological interpretation and application. In figurative terms they cry out *darshanee,* explain me. Why am I here? Dig into my depths and find out what I am trying to teach to you.

These comments show that the rabbis have searched for the meaning and the significance of the Tabernacle for centuries.

Interpretations

Everyone realizes there is some significance in the Tabernacle. However, many of the interpretations of the symbols that commentators, both Jewish and non-Jewish, ascribe to the Tabernacle are speculative and subjective, not objective. The most speculative see deep significance in every detail of the text; every tent peg, every dimension, every color—all ooze with spiritual importance.

For example, one book displays a poster-size drawing of the Tabernacle, printed in four colors and very nicely done. All the features of the Tabernacle are labeled. The four pillars to the entrance of the Tabernacle are labeled Matthew, Mark, Luke, and John. In other words, that is what the author interpreted the four columns to symbolize. This is an example of speculative interpretation. There is nothing in the text that tells us that the four pillars represent the four Gospels of Matthew, Mark, Luke, and John. In fact, those four pillars could just as easily have been labeled from Ephesians 4:11: apostles, prophets, evangelists, and pastor/teachers. There is just as little biblical warrant for doing that. Is there a particular meaning? If so, what is that meaning? How can we know?

1. INTRODUCTION AND OVERVIEW

The speculative approach to figuring out what each thing in the Tabernacle means spiritually can be fascinating intellectually. But its weakness is that most of such attempts to identify symbols lack biblical support. And without scriptural support for the symbol, we need to ask ourselves, "How do I know this is valid? Is this a genuine symbol? Is this a genuine lesson from God? Or is it the ingenious, speculative musings of some person's active imagination?"

We will not be speculative or subjective in our interpretation. We will always try to back up our statements with scripture.

Now we need to ask another question. "Does the scripture give us any guidelines for understanding the significance of the Tabernacle?" And the answer is "Yes!" The scriptures teach that the Tabernacle speaks first of the Messiah, and second, of scriptural, spiritual truth. Knowledge of the Tabernacle will lead us to a better understanding of the person and work of the Messiah and of the spiritual truths God reveals to us throughout His Word.

Let us take a closer look at this. First, what is the basis for saying that the Messiah is portrayed in the Tabernacle? The scriptural basis begins with John 1:14 in the *Brit Hadashah* (the Hebrew term for New Covenant). This is a very, very important verse.

> And the Word became flesh, and dwelt among us, and we saw His glory, glory of the only begotten from the Father, full of grace and truth.

We just read a very important word. The term is *Word*. *Word* is a reference to Yeshua,[3] to Jesus. Now John says that the Word became flesh. He is saying that the eternal God, the omnipotent, omnipresent, eternal God put on a body and came to earth and was found on earth as the man, Jesus of Nazareth.

---

[3] *Yeshua* is Jesus' name in Hebrew. The Greek form of His name is *Iesous*. "Jesus" is the rendering of the Greek form into English.

Then John goes on to say that He made His dwelling among us. That word *dwelling* (or the word *dwelt* depending on the version of the Bible you are reading) is the Greek word for *tabernacle*. It could just as easily be translated "He tabernacled among us." The word is a reference back to chapters 25 to 30 of the book of Exodus. A Jewish person reading that term would immediately think of this passage and realize John was talking about the Tabernacle of the Exodus.

Let us backtrack a minute. When we took our quick journey through the Tabernacle, we saw that the Holy of Holies was filled with the glory of God. The Hebrew word for the glory of God is *Shekinah*. The term *Shekinah*, or glory of God, is important because it is exactly how John goes on to describe Jesus. He says:

> ...and we saw His glory, glory as of the only begotten from
> the Father, full of grace and truth.

So just as God came to dwell in the midst of Israel in the Tabernacle, so now God once again comes to dwell in the midst of Israel in the form of His Son.

We have seen that the Tabernacle proclaims Jesus to be the Messiah, but will the Tabernacle also proclaim spiritual truth? Do we have a biblical basis to say that? Yes we do. Look at Hebrews 9:1-10. Hebrews 9:1a reads, "Now even the first covenant..." This is a reference to the Mosaic Covenant. Hebrews 9:1b continues, "...had regulations of divine worship and the earthly sanctuary." This is a reference to the earthly Tabernacle that we will be studying.

In Hebrews 9:2-4, the author now describes the Tabernacle in more detail:

> For there was a tabernacle prepared, the outer one, in
> which were the lampstand and the table and the sacred
> bread; this is called the holy place. Behind the second veil
> there was the tabernacle which is called the Holy of Holies,

> having a golden altar of incense and the ark of the covenant covered on all sides with gold, in which was the golden jar holding the manna, and Aaron's rod which budded, and the tables of the covenant;

These are all the items you looked at briefly on your tour through the Tabernacle. Hebrews 9:5-9a goes on to say:

> And above it were the cherubim of glory overshadowing the mercy seat; but of these things we cannot now speak in detail. Now when these things have been so prepared, the priests are continually entering the outer tabernacle performing the divine worship, but into the second, only the high priest enters once a year, not without taking blood, which he offers for himself and for the sins of the people committed in ignorance. The Holy Spirit is signifying this, that the way into the holy place has not yet been disclosed while the outer tabernacle is still standing, which is a symbol for the present time.

We will stop in the middle of Hebrews 9:9. Let us reread verse 9a again, "which is a symbol for the present time." This is the key verse telling us that the Tabernacle will provide us with spiritual truth. The remainder of verses 9 and 10 say:

> Accordingly both gifts and sacrifices were offered which cannot make the worshipper perfect in conscience, since they relate only to food and drink and various washings, regulations for the body imposed until a time of reformation.

We see that this Tabernacle was a symbol for the "present time" (meaning the time during which the book of Hebrews was written, before the destruction of the Temple). However, when the need for the Tabernacle ended, then it would be the time for it to cease. The Tabernacle would not always be there to constantly teach us.

An excellent verse to go to that verifies that the Tabernacle teaches us spiritual truth for the present day is 2 Timothy 3:16. In it, the writer, the Apostle Paul, confirms:

> All scripture **[including Exodus chapters 25 to 30]** is inspired by God and profitable for teaching, for reproof, for correction, for training in righteousness so that the man of God may be adequate, equipped for every good work.

And so we can learn spiritual truth from a study of the Tabernacle that will be profitable for us. It will teach us and reprove us when we are in error. It will correct us and train us in righteousness so that we can be well equipped to do God's work.

This is the approach we will take and the basis of interpretation that we will use. We have scriptural warrant for discovering what the Tabernacle reveals to us about the person and work of *Yeshua HaMashiach,* Jesus the Messiah, or Jesus Christ, which is the Greek translation of His name familiar to most traditional Christians.

In addition, it is valid to look for symbolic truths in chapters 25 through 30 of the book of Exodus. However, we will not do any detailed, speculative interpretations. We will limit ourselves to what the scripture has to say and to providing a biblical basis for any lesson or symbol that is shared. We will follow this principle: "Honor the silence of scripture as much as the statements of scripture." This principle is clearly laid out for us in 1 Corinthians 4:6:

> Now these things, brethren, I have figuratively applied to myself and Apollos for your sakes, so that in us you may learn not to exceed what is written, so that no one of you will become arrogant in behalf of one against the other.[4]

---

[4] *New American Standard Bible* (LaHabra, CA: The Lockman Foundation) 1995 update, (1 Corinthians 4:6).

Exceeding the statements of scripture is arrogant and promotes arrogance. We will refrain from falling into this mistake.

Format

Another area that we need to look at deals with the format that will be used. First, we will exegete the scripture and determine the basic meaning of the text. Second, we will look at the significance of the text, both historically and from a Messianic point of view.

What do we mean by looking at the historical significance of the text? We ask, "What did the text mean to the people to whom it was written, to the people who received it?" We do not want to impose 21st-century American culture on scripture.

American culture is linear in nature. It is precise, and it is technologically oriented. For example, when the very first space shuttle flight occurred, everybody was excited to see if the space shuttle would come down safely. Everybody was glued to the television as the space shuttle came into Edward's Air Force Base in California. It made a perfect landing! As the space shuttle rolled to a stop on the runway, a tiny clock on the screen was running. Called the mission elapsed time clock, it timed the mission in hours, minutes, seconds, tenths of a second, and hundredths of a second. Of course, that minute indicator didn't move very fast. The second indicator clicked away a second at a time, the tenth-of-a-second indicator ran more quickly, and the hundredth-of-a-second indicator was such a blur you could not read it. But just as the space shuttle wheel came to a stop, every digit on that clock stopped, including the hundredth-of-a-second timer. NASA was timing the flight down to the hundredth of a second. That is linear thinking. That is precise thinking. That is technological thinking. However, that is not the thinking of the scriptures.

The Bible was written from a totally different point of view. It is more cyclical in nature. The person to whom the message of the Bible was written thought in the sense of a cycle, the cycle of nature, for example, which is based on spring and summer, fall and winter. The ancients had technology, but nothing like what we have today. They did not have precise watches. They told time by the position of the sun. Their thinking was more approximate.

This cyclical perspective was typical of the person that received the revelation of the Bible from God. When we read the Bible through those eyes, through that grid, through those filters, we will get a clearer understanding of what God meant. That is the importance of taking a look at the **historical significance**. We will get a more accurate understanding of the truth God was trying to communicate if we look at it through the eyes of the person to whom it was given.

We will also look at the **Messianic significance** and will see how the scripture proclaims Jesus as the Messiah.

The final step will be to make an **application** from what we have learned. We will try to apply each section of scripture to our lives today. Why should we attempt to apply the scripture to our day-to-day existence? That question is answered in Hebrews 5:11 to 6:3.

The writer of Hebrews is talking about Melchizedek in chapter 5, verses 11-12:

> Concerning him we have much to say, and it is hard to explain, since you have become dull of hearing. For though by this time you ought to be teachers, you have need again for someone to teach you the elementary principles of the oracles of God, and you have come to need milk and not solid food.

The writer rebukes the hearers because time has elapsed. They have been believers for a while, and they have been taught from the scriptures. However, they seem to have regressed instead of moving along and gaining in their intellectual knowledge of scripture. They should be teachers of new believers by now, but instead they have to be taught again the elementary principles of the oracles of God. They have regressed through a lack of study, a lack of intellectual digging into the scripture.

Hebrews chapter 5, verses 13 and 14 goes on:

> For everyone who partakes only of milk is not accustomed to the word of righteousness, for he is an infant. But solid food is for the mature, who because of practice, have their senses trained to discern good from evil.

Now the writer makes a switch from the intellectual gaining of information to the application of scripture. Application is the solid food. You are trained by practicing scripture to discern good from evil. The people he is rebuking have actually regressed. They now have a harder time recognizing good from evil than they did before. The writer of Hebrews urges in verse 6:1:

> Therefore leaving the elementary teaching about Christ, let us press on to maturity, not laying again a foundation of repentance from dead works and of faith toward God,

You have already been taught those things; let us not go back and learn them all over again.

Picking up in the middle of Hebrews 5 verse 1 and going on through verse 3:

> ...not laying again a foundation of repentance from dead works and of faith toward God, of instruction about washings and laying on of hands, and resurrection of the dead and eternal judgment. And this we will do if God permits.

The writer is determined to move these Jewish believers on to maturity by teaching them to apply the scripture to their lives. He does not want them to just know the scriptures intellectually. He also wants them to practice the scriptures and learn to discern good from evil. These verses tell us that our walk with God is not an intellectual exercise or simply brain power. We are not to be walking Bible encyclopedias but to move beyond that point and live out what we are learning "in the trenches"! The result is spiritual maturity. The applications are designed to get you to move beyond head knowledge and into practical, obedient living on a day-to-day basis in the 21st century.

Four Temples

The next topic we need to touch on is the relationship between the Tabernacle and the Temple. This will help to short-circuit any confusion that a reference to the Temple might create in your minds. Simply put, the Temples of the Bible are permanent forms of the Tabernacle. The Tabernacle is the portable arrangement that traveled with Israel in the wilderness during the Israelites' journey to the Promised Land. When the Jewish people lived in tents, God also dwelt among them in a tent. However, when the people settled in the land and took up residence in permanent houses, then the Tabernacle gave way to a permanent arrangement as well. This permanent arrangement is called a Temple. The design and the lessons of the Tabernacle and the Temple are the same. The Tabernacle is the portable arrangement; the Temple is the permanent arrangement, both representing the same truth.

At this point, let us work our way through the Tabernacle and four Temples found in the Bible in chronological order, since some have already been built and some are yet to be built (see Figure 3).

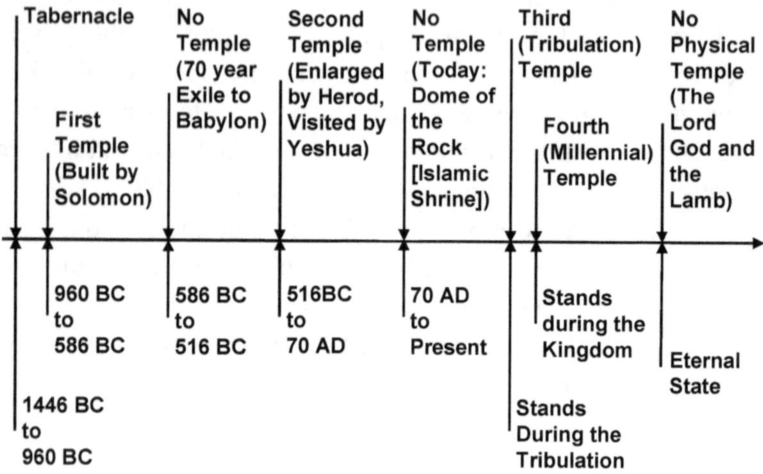

Figure 3. Tabernacle and Temple Timeline

Of course, the Tabernacle begins the sequence. The Tabernacle, the portable arrangement, was built in about 1446 BC, lasting for many years until 960 BC.

In 960 BC, the first temple was built. This was Solomon's Temple, which continued to exist until 586 BC when it was destroyed by the Babylonians. There was no Temple standing from 586 to 516 BC.

The second temple was then built in 516 BC by Zerubbabel. Zerubbabel built a small temple, but years later this small temple was enlarged and expanded by King Herod. It is Herod's Temple that we read about in the accounts of the Messiah's life. This temple is referred to as the Second Temple or Herod's Temple. We are talking about the same building begun by Zerubbabel and then enlarged and expanded by King Herod. This particular Temple was destroyed by the Romans in AD 70, and no Temple has been in existence from AD 70 to the present. The Temple mount has virtually been bare for

16

some 2,000 years. A few structures have been built on the Temple mount by various different religions, by the Romans and by the Crusaders. Today there is a structure sitting on the Temple mount that is an Islamic shrine known as the Dome of the Rock. It is a famous and well-known landmark in Jerusalem. But again, that is an Islamic shrine. No Temple exists there today.

Scripture teaches us that there is a Third Temple to come, and the best name for this Temple is the Tribulation Temple. This Temple will be standing during the Great Tribulation, also known as the Time of Jacob's Trouble. It will survive the Tribulation period, but it will not survive very long. Daniel 12:11 indicates that the Abomination of Desolation, which signals the Antichrist's takeover of the Tribulation Temple, will be removed 30 days after the end of the Tribulation period. The removal of the Abomination of Desolation indicates that the Tribulation Temple will come to an end at the same time.[5]

Finally, a fourth Temple will be built. This will be the Temple that will be built by the Messiah Himself. We will call this Temple the Millennial Temple, and it will exist during the thousand year Millennial Kingdom.

After the Millennium, or Messianic Kingdom, the Eternal State begins in which no physical temple stands. Revelation 21:22 tells us that the Lord God and the Lamb are its temple.

When a Temple is mentioned, remember we are referring to a more permanent version of the Tabernacle with the same spiritual truth that the Tabernacle teaches us.

---

[5] For more information on the Millennial Kingdom, see Dr. Arnold G. Fruchtenbaum's *Footsteps of the Messiah*, Part III, "The Great Tribulation," published by Ariel Ministries, San Antonio, TX, 2003.

Pictures

As we close this lesson, a disclaimer needs to be made about the pictures you will see illustrating the Tabernacle and its furniture. Exodus 25 through 30 is a very visual section of scripture, and it would be helpful to visualize exactly what the building looked like and exactly what the furniture looked like. Drawings can be helpful, but they have limitations. No one knows for sure what the Tabernacle and its furnishings really looked like. When you look at pictures in different books, you will see that they vary quite a bit, according to the understanding of each commentator. Remember, the pictures that you see are only artist's representations. Hopefully they are consistent with what the writer of the book of Exodus is describing. Keep in mind that variations introduced by an artistic illustration in no way reflect on the veracity of scripture. Scripture remains inspired by God. The Bible remains true and reliable.

Please do not sanctify any of the drawings. Remain flexible and open. Even though we do not know exactly what everything looked like, pictures can be helpful and are only a reflection of how a person with a 21st-century perspective views the data.

Likewise, while differences in opinion exist regarding the construction of the Tabernacle or the way the furniture was put together, these also reflect modern man's ignorance of the past. We do not have drawings or photographs or camcorder recordings of the Tabernacle. If we did, they would be 3,400 years old!

2. BIBLICAL PERSPECTIVES

GOLDEN RULE OF INTERPRETATION

It is very, very important for you to know our approach to interpreting scripture. You need to know where we are coming from so you can evaluate our teaching method and decide for yourself how accurate it is and how valid it is. We approach scripture from a position called The Golden Rule of Interpretation.

This rule, developed by Dr. D. L. Cooper, says:

> When the plain sense of scripture makes common sense, seek no other sense. Therefore, take every word at its primary, ordinary, usual, literal meaning, unless the facts of the immediate context studied in the light of related passages and axiomatic and fundamental truths indicate otherwise.

This rule may be a good one to memorize. Maybe it would help to break the rule down a little more and discuss what it is saying.

The Golden Rule of Interpretation begins by saying *when the plain sense of scripture makes common sense, seek no other sense.* In other words, assume that God is trying to talk to you through the pages of scripture in the same way that a writer of a book or a writer for the newspaper is trying to talk with you and communicate ideas. The writer wants you to understanding what he is saying. When it makes common sense, stick with the common sense. Assume that God is trying to communicate rather than hide information from you.

When the plain sense of scripture makes common sense, seek no other sense. Therefore, take every word at its primary, ordinary, usual, literal meaning. That means you are to take every word just the way you would take the words of someone writing a magazine article, a newspaper article, or writing a letter to you. Take their words in their normal, usual, literal meaning.

Then we come to a very important word *unless*. Now there are times we need to deviate from the primary sense or the plain sense of each word. That time comes when someone is speaking allegorically or symbolically to us. We take everything in the plain sense unless there is some indicator that the writer is not speaking to us plainly, but instead intends for us to understand the text from a symbolic or allegorical (figurative) sense. That information then has to come out of the context. The rule goes on, *unless the facts of the immediate context...indicate otherwise.* As you read scripture or as you read your local newspaper, you read it in the plain sense unless something jumps out at you from the page and says, "Wait a second. This is symbolic in nature. Do not take me literally." If that is what happens in scripture, then you have the warrant to move to an allegorical or symbolic interpretation.

We want to stress very highly that if plain sense is not possible, context is king. Plain sense is where you need to start, and then context is king. What do we mean by that? Context determines meaning. Many people criticize the Bible. They say, "I don't read the Bible. Nobody can understand it because you can teach anything you want to out of the Bible. You can teach anything under the sun." They have a certain amount of justification for saying that because many people do not make context king. They teach all kinds of things out of the Bible. The problem lies in the fact that the only way they can do that is to take the words of the Holy Scriptures out of context.

However, the Bible does not teach just anything in the world we want it to. The message from any given Bible passage is very precise if you keep each sentence in context. If you pull a phrase or sentence out of context, you can make it go anywhere you want, but you cannot do that if you leave it in its context. If it is in context, it only teaches one thing.

Here is a little example of what we are talking about. If we were critics of the Bible, we could claim that the Bible teaches there is no God. We could say that the Bible supports atheism and base that claim from three sections of scripture: Psalm 10:4, Psalm 14:1, and Psalm 53:1. All three of those psalms have sections where it says, "There is no God." Four little words, pulled out of context, do teach atheism.

There, we just proved it, have we not? No, because we have simply taken one phrase out of context. If you go to those sections of scripture, you will see a preceding phrase that makes the whole passage say, *"The fool has said in his heart,* there is no God." You suddenly see that the scripture is actually teaching exactly the opposite of atheism. The scripture actually teaches that a man or woman who is foolish in nature, who is irreligious in nature, who is sinful in their bent, who is a rebellious fool, that person wants to believe that there is no God. So they say there is no God in their heart. They want to be an atheist because they do not want to be responsible for their moral actions. That is a simple example of how context is king. If you pull a short sentence or phrase out of context, you can make it say anything. When you put it back into its context, the true meaning is clear.

With that in mind, the approach we are going to take will be The Golden Rule of Interpretation. Let us set the context for the Tabernacle found in Exodus 25 to 30.

Context

Context comes in many levels. It starts with a word, and a word fits in a phrase, and a phrase fits in a sentence, and a sentence fits in a paragraph, and a paragraph fits in a chapter, and a chapter fits in a book, and a book fits inside the Bible, and the Bible fits inside the culture of the day. All these various aspects of context have to be considered when we are teaching scripture, when we are digging into the meaning. We must seek to answer the question, "What did the passage mean to the people to whom it was written in context?"

We are now going to put Exodus 25 to 30 into its context. As the book of Exodus opens, the Jewish people are enslaved to Pharaoh. They are working with bricks and mortar, building Pharaoh's store cities. Eventually, Moses is raised up to be their deliverer in Exodus 2 to 11. Moses comes before Pharaoh nine times and says, "Let my people go." Nine times Pharaoh says "No!" Every time Pharaoh has a negative response, God brings a plague upon the house of Egypt. He brings those plagues upon Egypt for two reasons. First of all, He wants to teach Pharaoh who he is dealing with. Pharaoh does not know the Lord. God wants Pharaoh to know that he is not dealing with a frog god. He is not dealing with a river god, he is not dealing with a sun god, and he is not dealing with a fly god. He is dealing with the true and living God, the God of Abraham, Isaac and Jacob. He is dealing with an awesome and omnipotent God.

The second reason for the plagues comes in order to put pressure on Pharaoh. The plagues put pressure on him in order to get him to change his mind and let the children of Israel go free from slavery. Eventually, Moses comes before Pharaoh a tenth time. For a tenth time he says, "Let my people go"; and for a tenth time, Pharaoh says "No!" Now God brings the final plague, the tenth plague, and the most severe plague upon the house of Egypt: the death of the firstborn son.

Israel can escape that plague by obeying God and sacrificing a year old perfect lamb. They placed its blood upon the lintel and doorpost of each home. They retreated into their homes and spend the night in safety. That night God passed through the land of Egypt. When He came to the Jewish homes, the blood on the door indicated that a substitutionary, sacrificial death in place of the firstborn son had already occurred in that home. Therefore, God passed over the Jewish homes. When He came to an Egyptian house, no such blood marked the door, so God passed through the Egyptian house and struck the land of Egypt. The next morning, everyone in the land of Egypt felt the harsh sting of death. From Pharaoh on the throne to the most humble slave in the field, all had lost their firstborn sons. Israel was literally thrown out of the land the next morning. Unfortunately, Pharaoh soon repented of losing slave labor, so he sent his armies and chariots in pursuit of Israel. Again Israel was saved when God split the Red Sea, allowed the Jewish people to pass through on dry land, and then drowned the pursuing armies of Egypt. This is all found in Exodus 12 to 14.

In Exodus 19, after crossing the Red Sea and experiencing freedom from slavery in Egypt, Israel moved on to the base of Mount Sinai. Moses ascended Mount Sinai and received additional revelation and instruction from God. Moses received the Ten Commandments in chapter 20. Chapters 21 to 23 discuss various laws of the Mosaic Covenant. In Exodus 24, the covenant was confirmed, and then we come to Exodus 25 to 30 where instructions regarding the Tabernacle were given.

OFFERING FOR THE TABERNACLE

The first thing that God talks about in Exodus 25 is an offering that He wants collected for the construction of the Tabernacle. We find this in verses1 through 9, beginning with the nature of the offering in verses 1 and 2:

> Then the Lord spoke to Moses, saying, "Tell the sons of Israel to raise a contribution for Me; from every man whose heart moves him you shall raise My contribution."

We come across an important word in the beginning of this section. The word is *contribution*. In the Hebrew that word is *terumah*. *Terumah* is also the title for a particular section of the weekly Torah reading in the synagogue. What is a *terumah*? A *terumah* is that which is lifted off or separated. It is set apart from a person's possessions as a contribution. Notice the nature of this *terumah*, this contribution. It is voluntary. There is no command here. There is no amount specified. This is the key point. It is a voluntary contribution that comes from an eager heart, from a joyful heart. Raise the contribution for Me from every man whose heart moves him. It is given from a willing heart.

What was the content of the contribution? The answer is found in Exodus 25:3-7, beginning with verse 3:

> This is the contribution which you are to raise from them: gold, silver and bronze.

The contribution consisted of various items. We begin with precious metals of various worth. The first one mentioned is gold, and that is the most precious. Then, silver is mentioned. It is not as valuable as gold but still a very precious commodity. Finally, bronze is mentioned. This is the least valuable metal to be offered to the Lord.

We need to stop here and ask ourselves a question. Where did poor impoverished slaves get riches of this nature? Where did they get bronze, not to mention gold and silver? The answer to our question is found back at the beginning of Exodus, chapter 12. As we go back and look briefly at the Passover events, we read that the final plague had descended upon Egypt. Exodus 12:30-32 says:

Pharaoh arose in the night, he and all his servants and all the Egyptians, and there was a great cry in Egypt, for there was no home where there was not someone dead. Then he called for Moses and Aaron at night and said, "Rise up, get out from among my people, both you and the sons of Israel; and go, worship the LORD, as you have said. Take both your flocks and your herds, as you have said, and go, and bless me also."

Pharaoh gets Moses and Aaron up in the middle of the night and orders them to get out of the land. In verses 33-36 we read:

The Egyptians **[this is the common people of the land]** urged the people **[this is Israel]**, to send them out of the land in haste, for they said, "We will all be dead." So the people **[the Israelites]** took their dough before it was leavened, with their kneading bowls bound up in their clothes on their shoulders. Now the sons of Israel had done according to the word of Moses, for they had requested **[notice this is a request, not a demand]** from the Egyptians articles of silver and articles of gold, and clothing; and the LORD had given the people favor in the sight of the Egyptians, so they let them have their request. Thus they plundered the Egyptians.

So there is our answer. Where did the poor, impoverished slaves get gold and silver? They got the riches from their former masters, their former slave drivers, their former taskmasters, and they received these valuables upon request. Notice, it was not the spoils of war; it was not taken by force. It was urged upon them. In fact, it became their wages, the wages of slavery.

BIBLICAL SYMBOLS

At this point, we need to take a look at the biblical symbols being brought forth out of the text. We will spend some time establishing the meaning of these items. By doing it right now, it will provide a solid foundation for what we will be reading in the remaining chapters. We need to know what these symbols signified in the culture of the day. We will develop the meaning of these things out of the scripture themselves, out of the associations found in the Bible.

Gold

Let us begin with the gold. What are the associations centered on gold? Gold carried some of these associations in the Jewish mind of the Ancient Near East. Gold was linked to prosperity, to importance, to wealth, to position, and to royalty. We see an example of this in I Kings 10:1-2. The context here is the fame of King Solomon. His fame as a rich, wise, and magnificent ruler had traveled all the way down to the Queen of Sheba. In chapter 10:1-2, we pick up her reaction to the story she received about the wonder and wealth of Solomon.

> Now when the Queen of Sheba heard about the fame of Solomon concerning the name of the Lord, she came to test him with difficult questions. So she came to Jerusalem with a very large retinue, with camels carrying spices and very much gold and precious stones. When she came to Solomon, she spoke with him about all that was in her heart.

Notice that when this queen comes to visit King Solomon, a peer, she brings many, many items that speak of wealth. One of the things she brings is a lot of gold. The gold shows that she is prosperous, that she is important, that she is wealthy, and that she is of royalty. The gold is given to affirm the fact that she sees him as prosperous, important, wealthy, and of royalty as well.

We have a very similar association with gold today. Men like to wear their gold watches, and we like to have our fancy gold rings in 21st-century America as well.

Gold not only spoke of prosperity and importance, it also spoke of a fine and priceless character. Let us look at Job 23:10. Job was in the middle of a very serious and difficult time. He was being questioned by his friends who did not understand what was going on. Job responds to the comments of one of his friends. In verse 10, speaking of God, Job says:

> But He **[God]** knows the way I take; When He has tried me,
> I shall come forth as gold.

In other words, God knew all about Job. He knew what Job had done, right and wrong, and when He tries him, when He puts Job in the furnace of testing, Job will come forth as a very valuable person. God is speaking of Job's priceless character. Job's character will be refined, and he will be extremely valuable because of this, because of this trial that God will put Job through. So gold is associated with a very fine character.

Gold is also associated with a couple of other things in scripture. It is associated with power in Zephaniah 1:18 and with faith in 1 Peter 1:7. However, the most important associations we are looking at in our study of the Tabernacle are prosperity, wealth, position, royalty, and a fine character.

Silver

The second valuable metal that was collected for the Tabernacle was silver. Silver has very similar associations that speak of wealth and position. For that, take a look at 2 Chronicles 9:23-24. Here we have an association of silver with wealth and position. Chapter 9, again speaking of Solomon in verses 23-24, reads:

> And all the kings of the earth were seeking the presence of Solomon, to hear his wisdom which God had put in his heart. They brought every man his gift, articles of silver and gold, garments, weapons, spices, horses and mules, so much year by year.

Again, when these wealthy and important Kings sought out another King, another peer, another wealthy important man, they brought gifts commensurate with their position as a King and consistent with their position as a King. Silver spoke of wealth and position.

Silver also speaks of a fine character just as gold does. Look at Psalm 66:10. The context of the psalm is a time of suffering when the people are crying out to God. The psalmist says in verse 10:

> For You have tried us, O God; You have refined us as silver is refined.

The writer of this psalm realized that God was busy at work refining his character. That is what happens with silver and gold when it is put into the heat of the furnace. It turns to liquid, and that allows the dross—the impurities—to be drawn off. It is heated more, and again the impurities are drawn off. Every time it is heated, more impurities can be drawn off until it is finally pure. Refined gold and silver are mirror-like in their purity. Likewise with our character when God puts us through the heat of trials. He heats up the trial around us, and then He strips off the impurities until He refines our character, until we become something valuable in His sight. Silver speaks of wealth, position, and a fine character.

Go to the book of Proverbs, chapter 3, verses 13-14 for another association for silver. The writer of this proverb says:

> How blessed is the man who finds wisdom and the man who gains understanding. For her profit is better than the profit of silver and her gain better than fine gold.

Here silver is compared to wisdom. Even though gold and silver are both very valuable, wisdom is still better than the riches of silver and gold.

Bronze

Finally, we come to bronze. Bronze speaks of judgment in scripture. God says to Israel in Leviticus 26:18-19:

> If also after these things you do not obey Me, then I will punish you seven times more for your sins. I will also break down your pride of power; I will also make your sky like iron and your earth like bronze.

In other words, the earth will be dry and hard, and the Jewish people will be unable to plow it and plant their crops. God will make the earth like a sheet of bronze under their plow, and the result will be famine in the land. So bronze speaks of judgment.

Other associations with bronze are stubbornness, rigidity, inflexibility, and strength. For this, go to Isaiah 48:4 and Job 40:18.

In summary, gold and silver are given to kings by kings. They portray wealth, power, position, prosperity, fine character, and the fact that the person is of royal heritage. Bronze speaks of judgment.

3. MORE BIBLICAL SYMBOLS

BIBLICAL SYMBOLS

The book of Exodus includes other elements used as symbols, besides those of the three metals: gold, silver, and bronze. Colors, linen, goat hair, ram and porpoise skin, acacia wood, oil, spices, incense, and precious stones also have particular biblical associations.

Colors

In Exodus 25:3-5 we read:

> This is the contribution which you are to raise from them: gold, silver and bronze, blue, purple and scarlet material, fine linen, goat hair, rams' skins dyed red, porpoise skins, acacia wood,...

So the items we see brought forward now in verses 4 and 5 are blue, purple, and scarlet yarn to begin with.

What is the symbolism of these colors? Blue, purple, and scarlet cloth spoke of the best and most costly cloth. These were royal colors, as is evident in Esther 8:15, when Mordecai was going to be honored. Mordecai was the Jewish man who warned the king that he was going to be assassinated. His warning saved the king's life. Esther was Mordecai's charge, whom he had raised. She went into the king's court and became the queen of Persia.

Esther 8:15 says:

> Then Mordecai went out from the presence of the king in royal robes of blue and white, with a large crown of gold

> and a garment of fine linen and purple; and the city of Susa
> shouted and rejoiced.

Mordecai was honored with clothes of royal colors. Now turn to the book of Proverbs. Several associations are repeated in Proverbs 31:21-22. Chapter 31 describes the virtuous woman, the capable wife, the excellent wife, and we find out about her abilities in Proverbs 31:21-22:

> She is not afraid of the snow for her household, for all her
> household are clothed with scarlet. She makes coverings for
> herself; her clothing is fine linen and purple.

She makes the best for her family, this capable wife, this excellent woman. She clothes her family in the very best and highest quality of cloth available. The main idea behind these colors of blue, purple and scarlet yarn is that they represent the best cloth of royal colors.

There is also an association connected with the color scarlet. It is associated with permanence in Isaiah 1:18. God is speaking to His people here and He says:

> "Come now, and let us reason together," says the LORD,
> "though your sins are as scarlet, they will be white as snow;
> though they are red like crimson, they will be like wool."

A red color, when it stains cloth, is permanent. However, God contrasts the permanence with His glory and His grace. He says that even though our sins appear to be indelible, He can still make them white, as white as snow or like new wool. The great contrast of God's grace and our sin is brought out. We are aware of what happens when we spill some ketchup on a nice white blouse. The red stain is there permanently, just like a blood stain. Again, it is unlikely that you would ever be able to get it out. So the idea of scarlet is its permanence.

Fine Linen

Let us move on to fine linen. Fine linen in Hebrew is *shesh. Shesh* is fine white linen of exceptional quality. Commentators remark that this linen comes from Egypt and is of higher quality than modern linen because it has more threads per inch than a modern linen-making machine produces. That is the symbol behind the word *shesh*. It is an exceptionally high quality of linen and probably the kind of cloth that the woman in Proverbs used to clothe her family. She made clothing from the very best cloth she could buy.

Linen is also associated with righteousness, as in Revelation 19:7-8. The context is the Second Coming of the Messiah. Verse 7 reads:

> Let us rejoice and be glad and give glory to Him, for the marriage of the Lamb has come and His bride has made herself ready. It has been given to her to clothe herself in fine linen, bright and clean; **for the fine linen is the righteous acts of the saints [emphasis mine].**

Thus the saints are pictured as clothed with righteousness, and the passage points out the symbolism for us. *Righteousness* means living by a standard of behavior. The saints have lived their lives in a manner consistent with God's standards of behavior.

Goat Hair

Let us move on to the goat hair. It says in Exodus 25 that blue, purple, and scarlet cloth was gathered along with fine linen and goat hair. The goat hair came from longhaired goats, and most likely it was black in color. It was a very, very coarse or rough hair, the kind that was often used to weave tents. As we researched out this goat hair, we could find no particular symbolism for goat hair in the authorities that we consulted.

Ram's Skin, Porpoise Skin, and Acacia Wood

As we move on to Exodus 25:5, we see acacia wood listed. Acacia wood was a durable hardwood common in the Sinai Peninsula. As we researched out acacia wood, again we found no particular symbolism for acacia wood in the authorities that we consulted. The same is true for the rams' skins dyed red and the porpoise skins.

Oil

Exodus 25:6 continues:

> ...oil for lighting, spices for the anointing oil and for the fragrant incense...

There are many, many associations made with olive oil in the scripture. We will discuss just two important ones in this lesson.

The first one is dedication or consecration. Let us take a look at Leviticus 8:10-11. This is the consecration ceremony of the Priests. They are being set aside for their ministry as Priests in Israel. Leviticus 8:10-11 reads:

> Moses then took the anointing oil and anointed the tabernacle and all that was in it, and consecrated them. He sprinkled some of it on the altar seven times and anointed the altar and all its utensils, and the basin and its stand, to consecrate them.

When these physical items and the people were set aside for special use in the Tabernacle, they were then anointed with olive oil.

There is another very important symbol associated with olive oil, and that is the Holy Spirit. Isaiah 61:1, which is a Messianic verse, says:

> The Spirit of the Lord GOD is upon me, because the LORD has **anointed me** to bring good news to the afflicted; He has sent me to bind up the brokenhearted, to proclaim liberty to the captives and freedom to prisoners **[emphasis mine]**.

When the Messiah speaks about the empowering of the Spirit of the Lord coming upon Him, He associates it with anointing. Why is this? It is because He (God) has anointed Me (the Son), He has set Me (the Son) aside for special use. We will discuss anointing in just a moment.

Another very important association of olive oil with the Holy Spirit is found in 1 Samuel 16:13. David had been chosen as a replacement for King Saul, and now David is anointed and set aside for this new job that he will have. When David is set aside, we read in 1 Samuel 16:13:

> Then Samuel took the horn of oil and anointed him in the midst of his brothers and the spirit of the LORD came mightily upon David from that day forward. And Samuel arose and went to Ramah.

When David was set aside to be Israel's new king, he was anointed with oil. As soon as he was anointed, the Spirit of the Lord came upon him because the oil is a symbol of empowerment by God's Spirit.

Olive Oil. There are a lot of other symbols associated with olive oil, so we will just list them for you. You will have to study them on your own, but we will list the symbols with a cross-reference or two that will take you to each symbol and show you the association.

- We will look first at honor. Olive oil is associated with honor in Judges 9:9.

- Olive oil is also a symbol of joy in Psalm 45:7, Isaiah 61:3, and Proverbs 27:9.

- Favor and olive oil are associated in Psalm 23:5.

- Another association is fellowship in Psalm 133:2.

- Virtue and olive oil go together in Song of Solomon 1:3 and Ecclesiastes 7:1.

- Prosperity and olive oil are connected in Job 29:6.

- Olive oil also speaks of a change in status found in Ezekiel 16:9-10.

- The last association we found for olive oil is kind reproof in Psalm 141:5.

Anointing. Let us now take a side trip on the subject of anointing. Anointing comes from the Hebrew word *mashach*, meaning to anoint or to spread a liquid.

This word had an everyday use. *Mashach* could be used for rubbing a shield with oil. A soldier would rub his shield with oil to keep it in good shape and to perhaps encourage any object to slide off it that might get stuck on it. The term could be used for something as common as painting a house. It could also apply to putting oil on the body like suntan lotion or a skin softener. You would be anointing yourself with oil. That is the everyday use of *mashach*.

There was a religious use as well of the word *mashach*. There were actually two religious uses. The first was for ceremonial applications of oil on inanimate objects to consecrate them. We saw that when we discussed dedication in Leviticus 8:10-11 with the application of oil on the Tabernacle furniture in order to set it aside.

More frequently the word *mashach* was used in connection with ceremonial induction into a leadership office for a person. This was done by pouring oil from a horn onto the head of the chosen individual, the one who was going to move into this important office. So, by definition, this anointing oil became a tangible symbol of the setting apart of a man or things for God's service.

These associations generate four theologically significant points. The first point is the indication of authorized separation for God's service. This person was now in a position of honor which included increased responsibility.

The second point of anointing is the implication that God is the authorizing agent. Because God is the authorizing agent, the one who is anointed is now held in special regard because he is a representative of the King of kings and the God of gods.

The third theologically significant point lay in the fact that anointing implied that divine enablement would accompany the anointing. When a person was anointed, the expectation was that the Holy Spirit would come upon the person and enable him to do the task at hand. This was especially true if what the person was doing was of a religious nature, as in the case of the priesthood.

Finally, with anointing was an expectation of a coming, righteous, and spirit-filled ruler. This is what we saw when we looked at Isaiah 61:1. Again this is a Messianic verse:

> The Spirit of the Lord GOD is upon me because the LORD has anointed me.

Do you see the associations related to the oil? It stands for divine empowerment by God, and being set aside for special use by God, the authorizing agent.

We also see this in Luke 4:16-21. As we move over to the New Covenant, translated as *Brit Hadashah* in Hebrew, Jesus had come into the synagogue in Galilee and was teaching. He had been given the scroll of Isaiah the Prophet to read on *Shabbat* (the Sabbath day). He proceeds to read Isaiah 61:1, from the appointed section for that day. Verse 16 of Luke 4 reads like this:

> And He came to Nazareth, where He had been brought up; and as was His custom, He entered the synagogue on the Sabbath, and stood up to read. And the book of the prophet Isaiah was handed to Him. And he opened the book and found the place where it was written **[and here it is, Isaiah 61:1]**, "THE SPIRIT OF THE LORD IS UPON ME, BECAUSE HE ANOINTED ME TO PREACH THE GOSPEL TO THE POOR. HE HAS SENT ME TO PROCLAIM RELEASE TO THE CAPTIVES, AND RECOVERY OF SIGHT TO THE BLIND, TO SET FREE THOSE WHO ARE OPPRESSED,..."

So Jesus takes this picture and He applies it to Himself. Then He finishes up in verse 19:

> "...to proclaim the favorable year of the Lord."

And then in verse 20 of Luke 4:

> And He closed the book, and he gave it back to the attendant and sat down; and the eyes of all in the synagogue were fixed on Him. And He began to say this to them, "Today this Scripture has been fulfilled in your hearing."

When He wants to communicate that He has been set aside for God's special use as the Messiah, that He has been empowered by God, and that God has authorized Him to do this mission, He associates the whole idea of anointing and olive oil with that very moment. When the Messiah is set aside to do His mission of bringing good news to the afflicted, of binding up the brokenhearted, and proclaiming liberty to the captives and freedom to the prisoners, He reads the passage that associates His commissioning with olive oil and anointing.

Spices

The next item mentioned in Exodus 25 is spices. Spices were luxury items owned only by the rich. They were commodities that only important, rich and famous people were able to buy. They were luxury items for the prosperous. We see this association in 2 Kings 20:12-13. King Hezekiah is the King of Israel at this time and has been very sick, but God miraculously healed him. According to 2 Kings 20:12-13:

> At that time Berodach-baladan the son of Baladan, the king of Babylon, sent letters and a present to Hezekiah, for he heard that Hezekiah had been sick. Hezekiah listened to them, and showed them all his treasure house, the silver and the gold and the spices and the precious oil and the house of his armor and all that was found in his treasuries. There was nothing in his house nor in all his dominion that Hezekiah did not show them.

When these representatives from the kingdom of Babylon come to King Hezekiah in order to pay their respects, to honor him and to send him this get well card, the king gets a little arrogant. What does he show them? He shows them all the riches that he has, and one of those riches is spices. In 2 Kings 20:13 it says that he showed them his spices because he was a wealthy king and he liked to show off what he had.

Spices are also associated with physical attraction between a husband and his wife in Song of Solomon 4:10-16, 5:13, 6:2, and 8:14.

Incense

Incense, the tenth item in the passage, was collected for use in the Tabernacle. Incense was another extremely precious and extremely rare commodity. It was sought for its fragrance.

Incense is also associated with prayer. In Psalm 141:1-2, the comparison is made:

> O Lord, I call upon You; hasten to me! Give ear to my voice when I call to You! May my prayer be counted as incense before you; the lifting up of my hands as the evening offering.

This is a beautiful picture of a man standing there praying to God and raising his holy hands up to the Lord. It is a picture of incense rising in a fragrant column up into the heavens. The next time you pray, think of your prayers in this manner. Think of them as a fragrant column of incense rising up and dispersing into the heavenly realm. Your prayer is a fragrant and wonderful incense, a sweet aroma that God enjoys.

Precious Stones

Following in sequence, Exodus 25:7 continues listing the items that were to be collected for the construction of the Tabernacle:

> ...onyx stones, and setting stones for the ephod and for the breast piece.

This list summarizes the precious stones to be collected for use in the Tabernacle, and the symbolism of these precious stones is the same as for gold and silver. The association is with prosperity, importance, wealth, and position. Again, I Kings 10:1-2 would be an example. Let us look at that verse one more time:

> Now when the queen of Sheba heard about the fame of Solomon concerning the name of the LORD, she came to test him with difficult questions. So she came to Jerusalem with a very large retinue, with camels carrying spices and very much gold and precious stones.

When this queen comes to her peer, King Solomon, she brings gifts that are fit for her position and fit to be received by a person in his position, the position of king.

PURPOSE

That takes care of the items for the offering. God now explains the purpose for the offering and why these items were to be collected. Exodus 25:8-9 reads:

> Let them construct a sanctuary for Me, that I may dwell among them. According to all that I am going to show you, as the pattern of the tabernacle and the pattern of all its furniture, just so you shall construct it.

The purpose is to build a Tabernacle so that God might dwell among His people, His people Israel.

Three key words are highlighted in these verses. The first key word is *sanctuary*. It is a translation of the Hebrew *Miqdash*. This noun comes from the verb *qadash*. *Qadash* means to be hallowed, to be holy, to be sanctified, to be set apart, and not to be profaned. Now from that comes the noun *miqdash*. *Miqdash* is a holy place, a sanctuary, something devoted to the sphere of the sacred, something not to be profaned.

The next word is *tabernacle*. This word is a translation of the Hebrew *mishcan*. It comes from the verb *shakan*. *Shakan* means to dwell, to reside, to make one's home. From that we get the noun *mishcan*. The very important idea carried in these two words, *miqdash* and *mishcan*, explains the purpose of the Tabernacle. The omnipresent God, the God who is everywhere in the universe—not only on planet earth, not only with Moses—but also out in the far reaches of space, has chosen to reveal Himself at a specific location in His creation. This specific location is going to be in a Tabernacle—a tent—and, therefore, that location is set apart. It is sacred. It is not to be treated as common. This tent and this holy area are to be set aside and devoted to the worship of the God of gods, the King of kings, the omnipresent Creator of the universe. That is an amazing thought. God is going to cause Himself to be visible in this tiny, little pinpoint of a location.

We have another important word in verse 9 and that is the word *pattern*. This is a translation of the Hebrew *tavnit*. *Tavnit* means specification or blueprint. We come across the importance of this word by taking a look at Hebrews 8:4-5. The writer of Hebrews is talking about the priesthood and the High Priest. In verses 4-5 he says:

> Now if He were on earth, He would not be a priest at all, since there are those who offer the gifts according to the Law; **[Now he talks about the priesthood]** who serve a copy and shadow of the heavenly things, just as Moses was warned *by God* when he was about to erect the tabernacle; for, "SEE," He says, "THAT YOU MAKE all things ACCORDING TO THE PATTERN WHICH WAS SHOWN YOU ON THE MOUNTAIN."

Here we learn that the Tabernacle is a copy and shadow of the true Tabernacle that is in the heavenly realm. In order to portray the heavenly Tabernacle accurately, Moses is told to be sure and do all this correctly and responsibly and accurately. In fact, in the book of Hebrews, God warns Moses, "Do this right!"

Now move on to the next chapter of Hebrews, chapter 9:23-24, for another look at this idea which talks about Yeshua and His work:

> Therefore it was necessary for the copies of the things in the heavens to be cleansed with these, but the heavenly things themselves with better sacrifices than these. For Christ did not enter the holy place made with hands, but a mere copy of the true one, but into heaven itself, now to appear in the presence of God for us.

Here we see that Jesus and His work were done in the true Tabernacle. It was not in the copy or portrayal on earth but in the true Tabernacle in heaven. So the book of Hebrews teaches us that the Tabernacle to be erected, the Tabernacle that Moses is about to build, is a physical, visible copy of an unseen spiritual reality. In the book of Hebrews, it is called a type. It is called a *toopas* in the Greek. The definition of a type, a *toopas*, is "a person or thing prefiguring a future Messianic person or thing." We see why God wants Moses to be so careful and accurate. He is not to do a casual job. He is going to be portraying incredible, spiritual truth, so he has to do this properly.

Now we need to look at the significance of the offering, and what applications we can draw from the offering for us today.

HISTORICAL SIGNIFICANCE

We will begin by looking at the historical significance. Remember, the offering was a voluntary offering. It was voluntarily given as the very best that Israel had for their King. If the Jewish people were not willing to give it, then God did not want it. All the metals, all the cloth, all the oil, all the spices, and all the incense—all this was voluntarily given for the purpose of honoring and worshipping God. It was given for the purpose of praising the King of kings Who would dwell among them. He was being honored with the finest, most beautiful, most magnificent structure that Israel had the resources to make. Israel did not have the best in the world, but they brought the best that they had. They had just come out of Egypt. The splendors of the temples and tombs of Egypt far out-shadowed the Tabernacle in the amount of gold, in the artistry, and in the size of these incredible structures in Egypt. Israel could not compete with Egypt on that level. However, Israel brought the best that they did have to God, and they brought it voluntarily. By bringing it voluntarily, they would be exalting God, and in God's eyes, that kind of offering is the best kind of offering, the highest quality offering. God was saying to Israel, "Bring to Me the best of the best."

MESSIANIC SIGNIFICANCE

A very important Messianic parallel pertains to Israel's offering. The parallel is this: God voluntarily sent His best as well. God sent Yeshua, His Son, to dwell among the Jewish people. Yeshua is the best of the best. Take a look at John 1:14. As John describes Jesus, the Word of God, he says:

> And the Word became flesh, and dwelt among us, and we saw His glory, glory as of the only begotten from the Father, full of grace and truth.

The Word of God took up a human body and tabernacled among the people. John 3:16 highlights this as well. Verse 16 is probably the most well-known verse in all of scripture. It reads this way:

> For God so loved the world, that He **gave**...

There is that idea of voluntary giving:

> For God so loved the world, that He gave **His only begotten Son**...

There is the idea of quality, of the very best.

> For God so **loved** the world, that He gave His only begotten Son...

Did you catch the motivation there, too, of love? Voluntary giving of your best is an act of love because you want to do it, and we emulate what God did when we give Him our best out of love.

> For God so loved the world, that He gave His only begotten Son, that whoever believes in Him shall not perish, but have eternal life.

What a wonderful parallel. God did that for you and me that we might spend eternity with Him.

APPLICATION

The question we now need to ask is, "Do I give God my best? Do I give it to Him voluntarily? Do I give Him the best of myself?" In Romans 12:1, we are told to give God our very being:

> Therefore I urge you, brethren, by the mercies of God, to present your bodies a living and holy sacrifice, acceptable to God, which is your spiritual service of worship.

So, do I give God myself for His use?

Do I also give Him my material possessions to use? Again, we are looking at the collection of the saints. The Apostle Paul writes in 2 Corinthians 8:1-5:

> Now, brethren, we wish to make known to you the grace of God which has been given in the churches of Macedonia, that in a great ordeal of affliction their abundance of joy and their deep poverty overflowed in the wealth of their liberality. For I testify that according to their ability, and beyond their ability, they gave of their own accord, begging us with much urging for the favor of participation in the support of the saints, and this, not as we had expected, but they first gave themselves to the Lord and to us by the will of God.

Do you see the pattern there? If you give yourself to the Lord first—your very being for His use—then you will find it easy to give your material possessions. Do I give Him the best on my job, in my family, and in every aspect of my life? We may not have the best that the world offers, we may not be wealthy, but we can give to God the best that we have.

A great example of this is in the book of Luke 21:1-4. Jesus is in the Temple, and He is watching the offerings being put in the offering box in the Temple. This is what He sees in verses 1-4:

> And He looked up and he saw the rich putting their gifts into the treasury. And he saw a poor widow putting in two small copper coins. And He said, "Truly I say to you, this poor widow put in more than all of them; for they all out of their surplus put into the offering; but she out of her poverty put in all that she had to live on."

Again, this poor widow did not have the best that the world had to offer, but she gave to God the very best she had.

Finally, let us look at 2 Corinthians 8. The context is again this offering of the saints. Talking about the offering, Rabbi Shaul, the Apostle Paul, says in verses 11-12:

But now finish doing it also, so that just as there was the readiness to desire it, so there may be also the completion of it to your ability. For if the readiness is present, it is acceptable according to what a person has, not according to what he does not have.

The whole key of offering to God is willingness, the willingness of your heart. If you do not want to give to God, He does not want it. But if you do want to give to God, it does not matter what you give, just do it with a willing heart and give the best that you have. Paul says it is acceptable. You probably cannot give a million dollars to that project that would take the Gospel all over the world, but you can give one dollar or ten dollars, and God says that is acceptable because it comes from your willing heart.

The whole idea that is portrayed for us was not only for application in the construction of the Tabernacle, but it is also portrayed in the New Testament. Your offering is to be a willing gift, and it is to be voluntary.

4. CONSTRUCTION OF THE ARK OF THE COVENANT

BUILDING OF THE ARK

Let's look again at Exodus 25:10-22, and we'll explore the building of the Ark of the Covenant. We see a description of the ark in verses 10-16. Verse 10:

> They shall construct an ark of acacia wood two and a half cubits long, one and a half cubits wide, and one and a half cubits high.

The word translated ark can easily be translated chest or box. The dimensions of the ark or the box are given to us in cubits. A cubit was probably 18 inches in length. Literally, the word *cubit* is the word forearm. So a cubit was the distance from your elbow to the end of your middle finger.

Check out the length of a cubit using your own arm. Obviously it is not a very precise measurement! The society or culture in which the Bible was written was not nearly as technological as our culture is today. You can see that cubits varied in length according to the different lengths of each person's forearm. However, even though they were a much less technological society, they were still able to build items and build quite well, even using an approximate measurement. Archeologists have discovered that cubits varied from 18 to 25 inches in those days, but the standard cubit appeared to be approximately 18 inches.

So the Ark of the Covenant was just a small box approximately three feet, nine inches long, approximately two feet, four inches wide and approximately two feet, four inches high. What we have is just a plain, little footlocker. This is amazing. This most important piece of furniture, God's ark or box, is nothing more than a common, ordinary, plain box, no more, no less. How common. How ordinary. How disappointing!

Here we encounter a principle in scripture that is critically important for all of us to embrace. God is demonstrating that the common, ordinary, and plain can become uncommon, extraordinary, and significant when used in the service of God. This not only applies to small, wooden footlockers, it also applies to human lives. The common, the ordinary, and the plain *person* can become uncommon, extraordinary, and significant when used in the service of God.

Let's take a look at this little box, and we'll see how it is transformed from something very plain into something very beautiful.

Exodus 25:11 reads:

> You shall overlay it with pure gold, inside and out you shall overlay it, and you shall make a gold molding around it.

Overlaying the box with gold signified its association with the King. This is now something given to and used by a king. In this case, this little box will turn out to be the King's royal footstool. So, through the gold that was overlaid on the wood, the royal status and royal character of the King was displayed. This is no ordinary box. It is now fit for the King's service because it has been overlaid with gold.

The box is described as having a gold molding around it. In Hebrew the word is *zer*. It is a very accurate translation by both the New American Standard and the New International Version. This molding was simply a raised decorative edge that would locate and line up the cover that would go on top of the ark. It is nothing more than that. Unfortunately, the translation made in the King James Version (KJV) has led some people off on a very speculative track. The KJV translated this Hebrew word *zer* as crown. Because of that, commentators tend to wax eloquent about how this symbolizes the kingship of Jesus. The ark had a crown. Kings wear a crown. Bingo, this ark portrays Jesus as King. However, this word is never used of a king's crown, as a word study will show. This is simply a decorative molding around the top edge of the box. Do not read into it anything more.

Continuing in verses 12-15, we read about rings and poles:

> You shall cast four gold rings for it and fasten them on its four feet, and two rings shall be on one side of it and two rings on the other side of it. You shall make poles of acacia wood and overlay them with gold. You shall put the poles into the rings on the sides of the ark, to carry the ark with them. The poles shall remain in the rings of the ark; they shall not be removed from it.

This passage describes the method by which this portable royal footstool is going to be transported. In fact, that is what the box is going to turn out to be, a royal footstool. We will examine the idea of a royal footstool in more detail in an upcoming chapter. Because it is to be portable in nature, these gold-covered staves are attached to it so it can be lifted up and carried. Of course, the poles and rings are made in a manner consistent with the value of the item. They are all overlaid with gold.

CONTENTS OF THE ARK OF THE COVENANT

Golden Jar Holding the Manna

The contents of the Ark of the Covenant are now brought out in Exodus 25:16:

4. CONSTRUCTION OF the ARK OF the COVENANT

> You shall put into the ark the testimony which I shall give to you.

This verse indicates to us that something or some things should go into the box. What exactly was placed into the box is not detailed for us here; however, we do know the details if we turn to Hebrews 9:3-4. The writer of Hebrews is describing the Tabernacle, and at this point, the Holy of Holies. Verse 3 tells us:

> Behind the second veil there was a tabernacle which is called the Holy of Holies,

This is the 15 foot cubical room we read about earlier. Verse 4 goes on to say:

> ...having a golden altar of incense and the ark of the covenant covered on all sides with gold, in which was a golden jar holding the manna, and Aaron's rod which budded, and the tables of the covenant.

Hebrews tells us there were three items inside the ark. The first was the pot of manna. Now what is manna? Manna was the miraculous food God provided for Israel in the wilderness during the forty years of punishment while the Israelites wandered and were not allowed to enter the Promised Land. In Exodus 16:33, we learn that a jar was filled with manna and put inside the ark as a memorial for the generations to come.

Historical Significance

Let's look at the historical significance of the manna. The manna was bread from heaven, food from heaven. It was a miraculous, physical sustenance for the children of Israel. It's described in Psalm 78:24-25:

He rained down manna upon them to eat and gave them food from heaven. Man did eat the bread of angels; He sent them food in abundance.

Messianic Significance

For the Messianic significance of the manna, we'll turn to 1 Corinthians 10:1-3:

> For I do not want you to be unaware, brethren, that our fathers were all under the cloud and all passed through the sea; and were all baptized into Moses in the cloud and the sea; and all ate the same spiritual food.

This is a reference to the manna, which represents spiritual food. There is something more significant to the manna than simply feeding physical bodies for forty years. Jesus teaches us in John 6 what manna is—that it's more than just having a good dinner. The context of John 6 is that Jesus had fed the five thousand a miraculous amount of food a short time before, using just two fish and five barley loaves. The people who had experienced this miracle came to Jesus, and wanted him to do the same thing again. John 6:30 tells us:

> So they said to Him, "What then do You do for a sign, so that we may see, and believe You? What work do You perform?"

These people wanted Jesus to do another miracle for them, and they suggested what it should be in verse 31:

> Our fathers ate the manna in the wilderness; as it is written, "HE GAVE THEM BREAD OUT OF HEAVEN TO EAT."

In verses 32-34, Jesus responds to that request:

> Jesus then said to them, "Truly, truly, I say to you, it is not Moses who has given you the bread out of heaven, but it is My Father who gives you the true bread out of heaven. For the bread of God is that which comes down out of heaven, and gives life to the world." Then they said to Him, "Lord, always give us this bread."

They are thinking they are going to have free food forever. Then Jesus explains in verse 35:

> Jesus said to them, "I am the bread of life; he who comes to Me will not hunger, and he who believes in Me will never thirst."

Ah, so now we see that the manna represents spiritual food and that spiritual food is Jesus. We need to assimilate Him into our being in order to have spiritual life, just as we assimilate food and drink into our bodies to have physical life.

Drop down to verses 47-51 in John 6. Jesus elaborates:

> Truly, truly, I say to you, he who believes has eternal life. I am the bread of life. Your fathers ate the manna in the wilderness, and they died. This is the bread which came down out of heaven, so that one may eat of it and not die. I am the living bread that came down out of heaven; if anyone eats of this bread, he will live forever; and the bread also which I will give for the life of the world is My flesh.

When Jesus said, "This is the bread that came down out of heaven," do you think He might have been pointing to Himself? There is deep significance in the manna, deep significance in the fact that we need to take into our lives the death of Jesus on our behalf. It has to become personal; His death has to become part of us so that we can have spiritual life.

Finally, dropping down to verses 57-58, we read the words of Jesus:

> As the living Father sent Me, and I live because of the Father, so he who eats Me, he also will live because of Me. This is the bread which came down out of heaven; not as the fathers ate and died; he who eats this bread will live forever.

Do you think He is again pointing to Himself?

The bread in the wilderness, the manna, the miraculous sustenance was simply a shadow, a portrayal of the true sustenance that we are to receive when we place our trust in Jesus. Jesus is our true spiritual food. He is the true bread out of heaven. He is the source of eternal nourishment and eternal provision.

Notice, we started seeing in the beginning of the Bible, here in the book of Genesis, this concept of spiritual food; then we looked at it in the middle of the Bible with the Gospels; now it is also apparent in the book of Revelation at the end of the Bible as well. It is a theme that runs throughout scripture. This is the message to the church at Pergamum. Jesus says in Revelation 2:17:

> He who has an ear, let him here what the Spirit says to the churches. To him who overcomes, to him I will give some of the hidden manna, and I will give him a white stone, and a new name written on the stone which no one knows except he who receives it.

The overcomer will receive the hidden manna, the spiritual manna, the true life from Jesus. Spiritual sustenance or spiritual life is the reward for the believer, and the believer is the one who overcomes the trials, tribulations, and temptations of this world.

Aaron's Rod that Budded

The second item that was put in the Ark of the Covenant according to Numbers 17:8-11 was Aaron's rod that budded.

Historical Significance

This rod was a symbol of the priesthood of Aaron. The reason it was put in the ark was because Aaron's priesthood had been challenged. Therefore, Aaron's rod was placed in the ark as a reminder for generations to come that God had chosen Aaron, and there was no other family who had the right to priesthood.

Messianic Significance

The Messianic significance points to King Messiah as the future High Priest. Aaron was the High Priest under the Mosaic Covenant. But Jesus is the High Priest under the New Covenant. We see this in Psalms 110:4. The psalmist is not referring to David here. David was of the tribe of Judah; he was not of the tribe of Levi and could not become a Priest. This is not referring to Aaron either because he was of the Levitical order. Aaron is from the wrong order and David is from the wrong tribe.

Then whom is the passage referring to? Psalm 110:4 says:

> The LORD has sworn and will not change His mind, "You are
> a priest forever according to the order of Melchizedek."

This priesthood is under a different order than Aaron's. The psalmist is referring here to Jesus. He is the great High Priest who functions under the order of Melchizedek.

The writer of Hebrews, using an allusion to the Tabernacle, tells us that Jesus belongs to the order of Melchizedek—Hebrews 6:19-20.

This hope we have as an anchor of the soul, a hope both sure and steadfast and one which enters within the veil, where Jesus has entered as a forerunner for us, having become a high priest forever according to the order of Melchizedek.

The need for this new order of priesthood is explained in Hebrews 7:11-12:

Now if perfection was through the Levitical priesthood (for on the basis of it the people received the Law), what further need was there for another priest to arise according to the order of Melchizedek, and not be designated according to the order of Aaron? For when the priesthood is changed, of necessity there takes place a change of law also.

The need is there because the old order of Aaron was imperfect and limited. We needed a better order and a better priest. There had to be a change for the better. As a result Jesus is the new Priest under the New Covenant, under the order of Melchizedek.

In Hebrews 7:23-28 we read:

The former priests, on the one hand, existed in greater numbers because they were prevented by death from continuing, but Jesus, on the other hand, because He continues forever, holds His priesthood permanently. Therefore, He is able also to save forever those who draw near to God through Him, since He always lives to make intercession for them. For it was fitting for us to have such a high priest, holy, innocent, undefiled, separated from sinners and exalted above the heavens; who does not need daily, like those high priests, to offer up sacrifices, first for His own sins and then for the sins of the people, because this He did once for all when He offered up Himself. For the Law appoints men as high priests who are weak, but the word of the oath, which came after the Law, appoints a Son, made perfect forever.

Here the writer of Hebrews points out that the priesthood of Jesus and the order of Melchizedek are superior to the order of Aaron and the Mosaic priesthood.

Then he finishes with Hebrews 8:1-2:

Now the main point in what has been said is this: we have such a high priest, who has taken His seat in the right hand of the throne of the Majesty in the heavens, a minister in the sanctuary and in the true tabernacle, which the Lord pitched, not man.

There are a number of significant differences between the Tabernacle constructed by the people in the wilderness—the one we are studying right now—and the true Tabernacle. In the true Tabernacle in heaven, Jesus serves as our great High Priest. Man pitched the Tabernacle in the wilderness. God pitched the true Tabernacle in heaven. Man's Tabernacle is flimsy, weak, and needs improvement. God's Tabernacle is strong and perfect. Man's Tabernacle was served by sinful priests. God's Tabernacle is served by a perfect priest.

The rod of Aaron is a very significant item placed in the ark. It is symbolic of his priesthood and points to the high priesthood of Jesus, our Messiah.

Tablets of the Covenant

The third item in the Ark of the Covenant was comprised of the tablets of the covenant, mentioned earlier in Exodus 20, when Moses received the Ten Commandments on two stone tablets. These were placed in the ark, as we can read in Deuteronomy 10:2. What is the significance of the tablets of the covenant?

Historical Significance

Covenants of this nature, covenants between a king and his people—covenants between a suzerain (feudal lord) and his vassal—were common in the Ancient Near East. The Mosaic Covenant follows the standard structure for covenants of the Ancient Near East; in other words, when God makes His covenant with Israel, He makes it in a form that was understandable to Israel in the culture of their day.

Covenants in those days had six distinct parts.

The first part was the preamble identifying the king: This is who I am. We see that in the Mosaic Covenant in Exodus 20:2.

Next, the historical prologue recounted what the king had done on behalf of his subjects. We see the historical prologue brought out in the Mosaic Covenant in Exodus 20:2.

The third part contained the stipulations, or specific duties of the subjects. This detailed what the subjects would do in response to the benefit they had received from the king. The stipulations of the Mosaic Covenant are found in Exodus 20:3-17.

Next we move on to the fourth part of the Ancient Near Eastern covenants, the provision for deposit of the covenant. The covenants were deposited in the temple of the subjects and in the temple of the king. One copy of the covenant in the king's temple was for safekeeping, and one copy in the subject's temple was for periodic review. Periodic public reading of the covenant would be expected of the vassal people in order to remind them of all the stipulations of the covenant. We find the parallel for this provision of deposit happening in Exodus 25:16. In Israel's case, the Temple of the people and the Temple of the King is the same Temple. Since the two tablets of the covenant that Moses received up on Mount Sinai summarize the extended covenant, they were placed in the Ark of the Covenant. The Levites were expected to make copies and teach the people throughout the land what the Mosaic Covenant was about and what they were expected to do.

The fifth part is a list of witnesses that ratified the covenant. It said, in effect, "This is true. This is the agreement that the people and the king have entered into." The ratification of the Mosaic Covenant is found in Deuteronomy 4:26.

The final part of the covenant is a provision for cursings and blessings: curses for violation of the covenant and blessings for loyalty to the covenant. That is found in Exodus 20:5, 7 and 12, Leviticus 26, and Deuteronomy 28. This covenant form is visible in the Ten Commandments.

Messianic Significance

Is there a Messianic significance to all this? Yes there is. The Mosaic Covenant reminds us of a better covenant to come: the New Covenant.

We read in Hebrews 8:6-7:

> But now He has obtained a more excellent ministry, by as much as He is the mediator of a better covenant, which has been enacted on better promises. For if that first covenant had been faultless, there would have been no occasion sought for a second.

We see here that the New Covenant is the better covenant, the eternal covenant to come.

Chapter 8:13 goes on to say:

> When He said, "a new covenant," He has made the first obsolete. But whatever is becoming obsolete and growing old is ready to disappear.

Here the writer of Hebrews points out that the terminology of the book of Jeremiah, Jeremiah 31:31, speaking of a New Covenant, automatically shows that the first covenant is obsolete. The word "new" automatically means that what it is replacing is "old." The first covenant would be the Mosaic Covenant. It was conditional and temporary; it was ready to disappear.

Let's take a look at Hebrews 9:13-15, speaking about the priesthood of the Messiah:

> For if the blood of goats and bulls and the ashes of a heifer sprinkling those who have been defiled sanctify for the cleansing of the flesh, how much more will the blood of Christ, who through the eternal Spirit offered Himself without blemish to God, cleanse your conscience from dead works to serve the living God? For this reason, He is the mediator of a new covenant, so that, since a death has taken place for the redemption of the transgressions that were committed under the first covenant, those who have been called may receive the promise of the eternal inheritance.

There we encounter again a better covenant. The writer's mention of the New Covenant is, again, a reference to Jeremiah 31:31-34. Jeremiah 31:31-32 reads:

> "Behold the days are coming," declares the LORD, "when I will make a new covenant with the house of Israel and with the house of Judah, not like the covenant which I made with their fathers in the day I took them by the hand to bring them out of the land of Egypt, My covenant which they broke, although I was a husband to them," declares the LORD.

God very clearly states that the Jewish people did not keep the Mosaic Covenant. There is a problem here. We have a covenant that is impossible to keep and that is temporary and conditional. We need a solution to that problem because that covenant was broken very quickly by Israel.

Verse 33 goes on to tell the solution:

> "But this is the covenant which I will make with the house of Israel after those days," declares the LORD. "I will put My Law within them, and on their heart I will write it; and I will be their God and they shall be My people."

First of all this covenant is going to be individual. It is going to be within each person; it is going to be internal rather than external. Verse 34 continues:

> "They will not teach again, each man his neighbor and each man his brother, saying, 'know the Lord,' for they will all know Me, from the least of them to the greatest of them," declares the LORD, "for I will forgive their iniquity, and their sin I will remember no more."

Not only is there a strong emphasis on the individual nature of the New Covenant and how it is internal, there is a third important aspect. It deals with the sin issue. It provides forgiveness for sins. Indeed, it is a better covenant. It is also an unconditional and eternal covenant.

As we summarize the importance of this section regarding what was put in the Ark of the Covenant, we see the pot of the miraculous bread from heaven. The miraculous bread from heaven sustained Israel physically in the wilderness. It prefigured the true bread from heaven, Jesus, who sustains man spiritually. The second item in the Ark of the Covenant was Aaron's rod that budded. It prefigured Jesus, the greater High Priest. Third were the tablets of the covenant. These tablets represented the Mosaic Covenant and prefigured the better covenant, the New Covenant.

5. MERCY SEAT

MERCY SEAT DESCRIPTION

To this point we have looked on the outside of the covenant box—the Ark of the Covenant—then inside, exploring its contents. Now, let's direct our attention to the top of the box, the Atonement Cover, or Mercy Seat.

Let's begin with the description in Exodus 25:17:

> You shall make a mercy seat of pure gold, two and a half cubits long and one and a half cubits wide.

This verse gives us the specifics of the Atonement Cover, the Mercy Seat. It was a slab of solid gold, three feet eight inches long by two feet four inches wide. Remember, the ark had a molding around it. The cover would fit right inside that molding on top of the box.

The noun in the text is *kapporet*. Atonement Cover or Mercy Seat or place of atonement are all very acceptable ways to translate *kapporet*. *Kapporet* is from the word *kapar*. *Kapporet* is the place where the blood of the atoning sacrifice was sprinkled once per year on the Day of Atonement by the High Priest. (See Leviticus 16:14.)

The term Mercy Seat is related to the word atonement. The term also comes from the verb *kapar*. Atonement means reconciliation after enmity, reconciliation after hostility. Atonement is a satisfaction given for an offense.

What was the need here? The offense lay in the fact that our sins had created separation and hostility between us and our God. This fact is clearly stated by the prophets in the Bible. For example, we read in Isaiah 59:1-2:

> Behold, the LORD'S hand is not so short that it cannot save; Nor is His ear so dull that it cannot hear. But your iniquities have made a separation between you and your God, and your sins have hidden His face from you so that He does not hear.

In this section from Isaiah, Israel is suffering, and they want God to come and save them and pull them out of their predicament. God says, "Yes, there is a problem; your iniquities have made a separation, your sins have hidden My face, and I will not hear your prayer because of that." Hostility had been created between man and God, between Israel and her God, by sin. The place where God was reconciled to Israel was the Atonement Cover. When the blood of the atoning sacrifice was sprinkled on the cover, the atoning sacrifice satisfied God's wrath against sin. That happened once a year on Yom Kippur (the Day of Atonement).

However, we need to note that the satisfaction that was provided through the Yom Kippur sacrifice was only a temporary covering, a temporary covering over of the sins of Israel *until* the permanent and truly satisfying atoning sacrifice would be made (Hebrews 10:1-18).

The Cherubim

A description of the Atonement Cover is found in Exodus 25:18-21:

> And you shall make two cherubim of gold, make them of hammered work at the two ends of the mercy seat. Make one cherub at one end and one cherub at the other end; you shall make the cherubim of one piece with the mercy seat at its two ends. The cherubim shall have their wings spread upward, covering the mercy seat with their wings and facing one another; the faces of the cherubim are to be turned toward the mercy seat. You shall put the mercy seat

on the top of the ark, and in the ark you shall put the testimony which I will give to you.

The cherubim were not made separately and then fastened onto the gold cover of the ark; rather, they were fashioned as one piece out of the same massive slab of gold. They were one piece with the Atonement Cover.

Most drawings you see of the *cherubim* are rather poor representations of the real thing. Although we really do not know what these angelic creatures looked like, as we study the *cherubim*, we see that there are possibly three orders of these types of angels. There is an order of *cherubim* or angels with a single face. There seems to be another order that has two faces, and finally, a third order that has four faces. We believe it is the four-faced *cherubim* that were depicted on the Atonement Cover. We have a description of those *cherubim* in Ezekiel's vision from God that he describes in Ezekiel 1:4-14:

As I looked, behold, a storm wind was coming from the north, a great cloud with fire flashing forth continually and a bright light around it, and in its midst something like glowing metal in the midst of the fire. Within it there were figures resembling four living beings. And this was their appearance: they had human form. Each of them had four faces and four wings. Their legs were straight and their feet were like a calf's hoof, and they gleamed like burnished bronze. Under their wings on their four sides were human hands. As for the faces and wings of the four of them, their wings touched one another; their faces did not turn when they moved, each went straight forward. As for the form of their faces, each had the face of a man; all four had the face of a lion on the right and the face of a bull on the left, and all four had the face of an eagle. Such were their faces. Their wings were spread out above; each had two touching

> another being, and two covering their bodies. And each went straight forward; whenever the spirit was about to go, they would go, without turning as they went. In the midst of the living beings there was something that looked like burning coals of fire, like torches darting back and forth among the living beings. The fire was bright, and lightning was flashing from the fire. And the living beings ran to and fro like bolts of lightning.

Wow, what a description! Here, they are only identified as living creatures, but in Ezekiel 10:1, we get a positive identification of them. Ezekiel again has a vision:

> Then I looked, and behold, in the expanse that was over the heads of the cherubim something like a sapphire stone, in appearance resembling a throne, appeared above them.

Ezekiel now names them as the *cherubim*. He also does the same in Ezekiel 10:15 as he describes what he sees:

> Then the cherubim rose up. They are the living beings that I saw by the river Chebar.

Here is a very distinct identification. The living beings that we saw in Ezekiel 10:1 are the *cherubim*, and the positive identification is in Ezekiel 10:15.

Purpose of the Cherubim

Now what was the purpose of the *cherubim*, these incredible creatures? In Ezekiel 1:25-28, we learn why these creatures have been created:

> And there came a voice from above the expanse that was over their heads; whenever they stood still, they dropped

their wings. Now above the expanse that was over their heads there was something resembling a throne, like lapis lazuli in appearance; and on that which resembled a throne, high up, was a figure with the appearance of a man. Then I noticed from the appearance of His loins and upward something like glowing metal that looked like fire all around within it, and from the appearance of His loins and downward I saw something like fire; and there was a radiance around Him. As the appearance of the rainbow in the clouds on a rainy day, so was the appearance of the surrounding radiance. Such was the appearance of the likeness of the glory of the LORD. And when I saw it, I fell on my face and heard a voice speaking.

This short description tells us the *cherubim* are the attendants of the throne of God. They are God's glorious throne attendants. They are part of God's footstool. God's throne appears in the expanse above them. This is also confirmed in Psalms 80:1. The psalmist, Asaph, is crying out to God, and he says in verse 1:

Oh, give ear, Shepherd of Israel, You who lead Joseph like a flock; You who are enthroned above the cherubim, shine forth!

The Ark of the Covenant where the *cherubim* dwell is God's footstool, the footstool of his throne. The Ark of the Covenant in the Tabernacle prefigures the true footstool in the heavenly realms. The golden *cherubim* on the Ark of the Covenant in the Tabernacle are only likenesses, mere shadows, mere representations of the true *cherubim* that are part of God's footstool in the heavenly realms.

PURPOSE OF THE ARK

Exodus 25:22 reveals the purpose for the ark and the Mercy Seat:

There I will meet with you; and from above the mercy seat, from between the two cherubim which are upon the ark of the testimony, I will speak to you about all that I will give you in commandment for the sons of Israel.

Figure 4. The Mercy Seat

We see that Israel's King will meet with His people here, at the ark and Mercy Seat (see Figure 4). Moses has just learned that he is creating a throne room as he builds the tabernacle—the throne room for God Almighty.

Historical Significance

First, this is the place where the King of kings would meet with His people and deal with their sins and receive worship. The ark was the footstool of the throne of God where the presence of God would be visibly seen between the *cherubim.* Turn to Psalms 99:1-5 to read about the ark and the Mercy Seat in that context:

> The LORD reigns, let the peoples tremble; He is enthroned *above* the cherubim, let the earth shake! The LORD is great in Zion, and He is exalted above all the peoples. Let them praise Your great and awesome name; Holy is He. The strength of the king loves justice; You have established equity; You have executed justice and righteousness in Jacob. Exalt the LORD our God and worship at His footstool; Holy is He.

Next, the ark and the Mercy Seat were where the sins were covered over. Leviticus 16:14-17 describes the Day of Atonement and duties of the High Priest:

> Moreover, he shall take some of the blood of the bull and sprinkle it with his finger on the mercy seat on the east side; also in front of the mercy seat he shall sprinkle some of the blood with his finger seven times. Then he shall slaughter the goat of the sin offering which is for the people, and bring its blood inside the veil and do with its blood as he did with the blood of the bull, and sprinkle it on the mercy seat and in front of the mercy seat. He shall make atonement for the holy place, because of the impurities of the sons of Israel and because of their transgressions in regard to all their sins; and thus he shall do for the tent of meeting which abides with them in the midst of their impurities. When he goes in to make atonement in the holy place, no one shall be in the tent of meeting until he comes

out, that he may make atonement for himself and for his household and for all the assembly of Israel.

The High Priest would go into the Holy of Holies and sprinkle the blood on the Ark of the Covenant, on the Atonement Cover, and here satisfaction and reconciliation for sin would occur.

Messianic Significance

The Messianic significance of the Ark of the Covenant and the Atonement Cover lies in the fact that we, too, can come into God's throne room. We can come into the very presence of God because of our relationship with *Yeshua*. In ancient Israel, only the High Priest could come into the very presence of God in the Holy of Holies; but you and I, as believers in *Yeshua*, have received that same privilege.

Speaking of the High Priest, the writer of Hebrews 4:14-16 says:

> Therefore, since then we have a great high priest who has passed through the heavens, Jesus the son of God, let us hold fast our confession. For we do not have a high priest who cannot sympathize with our weaknesses, but One who has been tempted in all things as *we are, yet* without sin. Therefore let us draw near with confidence to the throne of grace, so that we may receive mercy and find grace to help in time of need.

Scripture tells us that when we come in prayer to God, we are coming into the very throne room of God. We can approach God's throne today because of our relationship with *Yeshua*. And that is an incredible thought! But it does not stop there. We will even get to share his throne as co-rulers. Look in Revelation 3:21. This is where John writes the words of Messiah's message to the church in Laodicea:

> He who overcomes, I will grant to him to sit down with Me
> on My throne, as I also overcame and sat down with My
> Father on His throne.

The overcomer is the one who places his faith in Jesus and receives the gift of eternal life. The overcomers receive a promise that they will sit on *Yeshua's* throne; they will be co-rulers with Him when He rules over this planet during the Messianic Kingdom. The first item of Messianic significance is that you and I can come into God's throne room; and not only that, we will share His throne as co-rulers in the future because we are the overcomers.

There is another item of Messianic significance. The wrath of God which burned against sin demanded that punishment be exacted. That is a principle throughout scripture, and the appropriate punishment was the death of the sinner. That is bad news. But there is good news: God is willing to accept a substitute. In the face of this principle of God's wrath burning against sin and demanding punishment, we find that the death of the Messiah was the substitutionary punishment that satisfied the holy demands of a righteous God. Therefore, God is reconciled to the believer. God is reconciled to you and me through *Yeshua's* substitutionary atonement, His substitutionary punishment. We see this in 1 John 2:1-2:

> My little children, I am writing these things to you so that
> you may not sin. And if anyone sins, we have an Advocate
> with the Father, Jesus Christ the righteous; and He Himself
> is the propitiation for our sins; and not for ours only, but
> also for those of the whole world. [*Propitiation* is a Latin
> word that indicates the means of forgiveness.]

Jesus is not only the personal source of satisfaction, that atoning sacrifice, but He is also our source of reconciliation. We see that in Romans 5:10-11:

> For if while we were enemies we were reconciled to God through the death of His Son, much more, having been reconciled, we shall be saved by His life. And not only this, but we also exalt in God through our Lord Jesus Christ, through whom we have now received the reconciliation.

Application

We need to ask ourselves, "Have I been reconciled to God?" As you read this chapter, you may have suddenly realized that this has not occurred. Reconciliation occurs by simply recognizing that there is bad news—that there is a problem in your life—and the problem is the sin issue. The issue of sin has to be dealt with. God demands the death of the sinner because His wrath burns against sin. That is the first step, to recognize the bad news.

The second step is to recognize the good news. The message of the New Covenant is that Jesus is our atoning sacrifice. He is our source of forgiveness, and He is our source of reconciliation when we place our faith in Him. When we receive His work on our behalf personally, then God counts our sins as forgiven. God's wrath against our sin is satisfied because Jesus, as the substitute, takes the punishment, and we are free. We can now enter into a personal relationship with God. We are reconciled to God.

If you realize after reading this chapter that you have not received reconciliation from God, that God is not satisfied with you, we would urge you to turn to Jesus in faith at this moment and receive Him into your life as your Savior and be reconciled to God. You can do that through prayer. Read the following prayer, and if these words reflect your heart, just speak them out to God. However, you don't have to use our words. You just need words that express the thoughts of your heart. Bow your heart before God and either use words of your own or these words:

Dear Father, God of Abraham, Isaac and Jacob. I realize that I stand under Your wrath because of my sin. I am a sinner in need of forgiveness, and You are not satisfied with my life. I have fallen short of Your glory, and I see, Lord, that I can't make things right on my own. I need help to satisfy you. And I've learned that Jesus is my source of satisfaction, my source of reconciliation. He is the substitutionary sacrifice, and Your punishment has fallen upon Him, and I want to acknowledge that. Lord, that is what I want: forgiveness from You. I need a substitute. I understand and submit myself to the fact that Jesus is my substitute. I want to receive Jesus as my Savior. I want to receive the gift of eternal life that You promised to me. Father, I repent of my sins. I change my mind about my sins. I want to live a new life from this point on with Your spirit within me, guiding me in this new life. I want to know Your Word and follow You. Father, help me to grow now that I've received Jesus as my Savior and the gift of eternal life. Thank you for saving me and loving me. Amen.

6. TABLE OF SHOWBREAD AND LAMP STAND

TABLE OF SHOWBREAD DESCRIPTION

The Table of Showbread is described in Exodus 25:23-30. Verses 23-25 read:

> You shall make a table of acacia wood, two cubits long and one cubit wide and one and a half cubits high. You shall overlay it with pure gold and make a gold border around it. You shall make for it a rim of a handbreadth around *it*; and you shall make a gold border for the rim around it.

We discover that the table is a very small table about three feet long, one and a half feet wide and about two feet high (see Figure 5). It is just a low, little table, perhaps the size of a coffee table. However, we are told that it is overlaid with pure gold, so it is a worthy gift for the King. A piece of furniture that belongs in a King's throne room, it is again the best that Israel has to offer.

We read that there are two moldings associated with the table, although no one is exactly sure what they are like. There are two options. First, there was perhaps an outer and an inner molding; the outer molding was around the outside edge of the table and the inner molding was maybe a raised lip, locating where the Bread of the Presence, the showbread, would be placed.

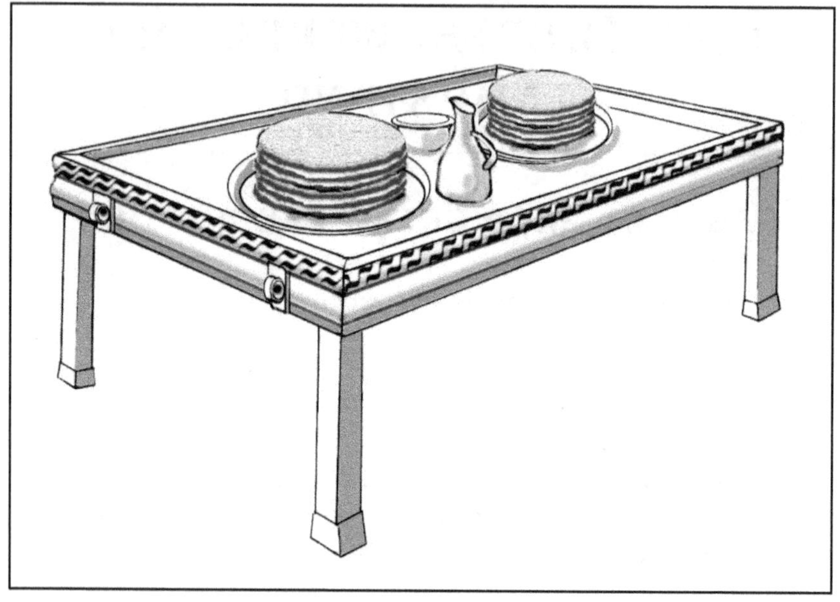

Figure 5. Table of Showbread

The second option is an outer lip that would be the molding and a rung between the legs of the table to strengthen the legs and to keep the table from being wobbly.

Transportable

The table, like everything else in the Tabernacle, was portable. Exodus 25:26-28 tells us:

> You shall make four gold rings for it and put rings on the four corners which are on its four feet. The rings shall be close to the rim as holders for the poles to carry the table. You shall make the poles of acacia wood and overlay them with gold, so that with them the table may be carried.

These rings and poles were made for carrying it.

Accessories

The various utensils are described for us in Exodus 25:29:

> You shall make its dishes and its pans and its jars and its
> bowls with which to pour drink offering; you shall make
> them of pure gold.

The accessories for the operation of the Table of Showbread are to be made of gold, the highest quality material.

In verse 29, the rabbis feel that the words jars and bowls actually describe some tubular supports and platforms that carried the bread. We do not know exactly what the Table of Showbread was like, so there are a variety of different interpretations. If you see drawings that look very different, please keep in mind that it is 21st-century human ignorance that is the culprit and not anything related to the Word of God.

Bread of Presence

Why would God have Israel construct the Table of Showbread? The purpose for the table is found in verse 30:

> You shall set the bread of the Presence on the table before
> Me at all times.

The table has been constructed to hold the Bread of the Presence continually before the LORD. Now the word "Presence" here refers to the presence of God. The word literally means face-to-face, face-to-face with God. The rabbis feel, however, that this description of the Bread of the Presence actually refers to the shape of the bread rather

Figure 6. The Showbread (A Rabbinic Opinion)

than the presence of God. In the rabbis' reconstruction of the bread, they conceive of the bread as being C-shaped with the two points of the "C" facing each other (see Figure 6). One face is looking at the other face. They felt that was the reason it was called the Bread of the Presence or bread of the faces.

The actual bread that was put on the table along with its recipe is described for us in Leviticus 24:5-8:

> Then you shall take fine flour and bake twelve cakes with it; two-tenths *of an ephah* shall be in each cake. You shall set them in two rows, six to a row, on the pure *gold* table

before the LORD. You shall put pure frankincense on each row that it may be a memorial portion for the bread, *even* an offering by fire to the LORD. Every Sabbath day he shall set it in order before the LORD continually; it is an everlasting covenant for the sons of Israel. It shall be for Aaron and his sons, and they shall eat it in a holy place; for it is most holy to him from the LORD'S offerings by fire, *his* portion forever.

Thus 12 loaves were baked, one for each tribe, and they were a perpetual offering to the LORD. They were placed on the table each Sabbath and left there until the following Sabbath. Then on the following Sabbath, the loaves were removed and eaten by the priests. These 12 loaves were arranged in two rows of six loaves each. Frankincense, an incense, was placed on the table and burned either in small piles beside the loaves or perhaps in small bowls alongside the loaves.

Historical Significance

The bread and frankincense was a memorial offering in three ways. First, bread was regarded as the mainstay of man's nourishment. So the bread on the table is symbolic of man's need, the need for food in order to survive. This is a very common picture in scripture. Jesus, for example, used bread as a symbol of nourishment. In Matthew 6:11, in the very famous Lord's Prayer, He says, "give us today our daily bread."

This expression does not mean that we are asking God simply for bread everyday but for our basic, daily, physical sustenance. The bread is a reminder that God provides for us on a daily basis.

Second, the bread emphasized the concept of communion or fellowship. In ancient Israel, hospitality was a highly-esteemed virtue. It was an honor to provide for a guest. Eating with another person wasn't a casual affair but rather an important part of the day. It communicated friendship, acceptance, fellowship and the desire for a quality relationship.

The third item that was being memorialized is prayer. Frankincense is a symbol of prayer. This is a reminder to Israel that she needs to experience fellowship with God. Israel experiences sustenance from God through prayer. We depend upon God for all we need.

In summary, the table and the Bread of the Presence were a memorial offering, a reminder that God sustains his people. He desires their communion, their fellowship, and their prayers.

Messianic Significance

To understand Messianic significance of the Table of Showbread, let's turn to the Hertz *Pentateuch.* The following is a comment by the well-known and respected Jewish commentator, Maimonides. In regard to the Table of Showbread, he confesses:

> (I)…do not know the object of the table with the bread upon it continually, and to this day I have not be able to assign any reason to this commandment.

What a sad statement. One of the greatest rabbinic commentators does not know the reason behind the table and the bread, and he has no idea why God gave this commandment. Two Messianic concepts are memorialized and taught through the Table of Showbread.

First, the Table of Showbread signified that *Yeshua* is the bread of life. *Yeshua* is the one who sustains us and nourishes us, and He is the one with whom we have intimate fellowship. Let us take a look at John 6:35:

> Jesus said to them, "I am the bread of life; he who comes to Me will not hunger, and he who believes in Me will never thirst."

We are to come to Jesus, and assimilate Him just the way we assimilate bread. Just as bread nourishes our body and provides us with physical life, assimilating Jesus will bring spiritual life. We will not have spiritual hunger anymore when we have intimate fellowship with Him. He is the bread of life, the true life. This whole idea is also repeated for us in Revelation 3:20. There Jesus said:

> Behold, I stand at the door and knock; if anyone hears My voice and opens the door, I will come in to him and will dine with him, and he with Me.

Revelation 3:20 is often used as an evangelistic verse, signifying that Jesus is standing at the door of the unbeliever's heart and He knocks on the door. If the unbeliever allows Him to come in, the unbeliever is saved.

However, others feel that Revelation 3:20 is written to believers. He is knocking on the door of a believer's heart. He is saying He wants to have fellowship with us. *Let Me into your life. Make Me the Lord of your life so that I can dine with you and you with Me, and we can have intimate fellowship together.*

The showbread, as well as the manna inside the Ark of the Covenant, has very similar associations. Just as the bread symbolized provision for daily, physical need, so Yeshua, the bread of life, is our provision for daily spiritual needs. He desires our fellowship, and He sustains us daily.

There is a second lesson pictured here. The life of Jesus was characterized by prayer. Remember, frankincense was burned upon the Table of Showbread, and the frankincense is a symbol of prayer.

In the New Covenant or the New Testament, there are lots of examples of Jesus praying. We get a glimpse of the prayer life of the Messiah in Luke 6:12:

> It was at this time that He went off to the mountain to pray, and He spent the whole night in prayer to God.

He could spend eight to twelve hours in prayer to God. That is really convicting! Jesus was truly a man of prayer.

Application

We do not want this book to be purely an academic pursuit. We need to apply it to our daily walk and ask ourselves some questions. The first, "Do I set aside adequate time for devotions and prayer so I can grow in my fellowship with *Yeshua*? I want to have that intimate time with Him that He so desires for me to have. Is He knocking on the door of my heart? Will I let Him in?"

A second question would be, "Is He my bread of life? Does He sustain me moment by moment, day to day? Do I seek Him often; do I seek Him earnestly? Or do I view Him as a spiritual life preserver when I am in trouble? Do I walk with Him day by day, or do I limit my prayers to cries for help?" It is great to cry out to the Lord for help, and He will be there, but He desires to be so much more than that.

Look at Ephesians 6:18-19 and ask yourself, "Does this passage characterize my life?"

> With all prayer and petition pray at all times in the Spirit, and with this in view, be on the alert with all perseverance and petition for all the saints, and *pray* on my behalf, that utterance may be given to me in the opening of my mouth, to make known with boldness the mystery of the gospel...

Rabbi Shaul, the Apostle Paul, tells us to pray at all times in the Spirit, to be alert, to pray for the saints, to pray for him, to pray for each other, and to pray for our pastors. That should characterize our lives. Am I growing in my knowledge of Him?

LAMP STAND DESCRIPTION

As we approach the end of Exodus 25, we come to the next piece of furniture in the Holy Place of the Tabernacle. The lamp stand (see Figure 7) is described for us in Exodus 25:31-40, with the physical description in verses 31-36:

> Then you shall make a lamp stand of pure gold. The lamp stand *and* its base and its shaft are to be made of hammered work; its cups, and its bulbs and its flowers shall be *of one piece* with it. Six branches shall go out from its side; three branches of the lamp stand from its one side and three branches of the lamp stand from its other side. Three cups *shall be* shaped like almond *blossoms* in the one branch, a bulb and a flower, and three cups shaped like almond *blossoms* in the other branch, a bulb and a flower— so for six branches going out from the lamp stand; and in the lamp stand four cups shaped like almond *blossoms*, its bulbs and its flowers. A bulb shall be under the *first* pair of branches *coming* out of it, and a bulb under the *second* pair of branches coming out of it, and a bulb under the *third* pair of branches *coming* out of it, for the six branches coming out of the lamp stand. Their bulbs and their branches *shall be of one piece* with it; all of it shall be one piece of hammered work of pure gold.

Figure 7. The Lamp Stand

You will notice that no dimensions are given for this article of furniture. We do not know exactly how large it was. We do have Jewish tradition to go by, however. Jewish tradition gives us a height for the lamp stand of about five feet. The width would be about three-and-one-half feet. Probably the most accurate drawing or reproduction of the Tabernacle with the lamp stand is found on the Arch of Titus in Rome. That drawing was part of a scene that depicted the fall of the Temple. We cannot be sure that the lamp stand looked exactly like that picture, but at least it would be similar. Like the other pieces of furniture, it was made of the best that Israel had to offer. It was made of pure gold, and therefore, it was a worthy gift for the King of kings.

The reason the lamp stand was constructed in this manner is given in Exodus 25:37:

> Then you shall make its lamps seven *in number;* and they shall mount its lamps so as to shed light on the space in front of it.

The lamp stand was the only source of light in the Holy Place. Ancient lamps were simply a small clay bowl that had been pinched in on one side and then fired. The wick was laid in the pinched-in area with the bottom of the wick in the oil and the top protruded so it could be lit.

According to Exodus 30:8, and possibly 1 Samuel 3:3, the lamp stand was lit at night and extinguished in the morning. However, there is a debate over the time that the lamp stand burned. Did it burn 24 hours or only at night? The debate comes from the fact that some commentators feel that Exodus 27:20 implies that the lamps burnt continually and never went out. You will find both positions in commentaries.

The Soncino commentary (page 519) handles the issue this way:

> *continually.* i.e. 'regularly,' night after night (R, E). The central lamp was to burn continually, and from it the others were kindled each evening (N).

The accessories used for the functioning of the lamp stand are described in Exodus 25:38-40:

> The snuffers and their trays *shall be* of pure gold. It shall be made from a talent of pure gold, with all these utensils. See that you make *them* after the pattern for them, which was shown you on the mountain.

The other articles necessary for the functioning of the lamp stand were made with the same attention to quality; they were made out of pure gold. The lamp stand itself was made of one talent of pure gold, which equals approximately 75 pounds of gold. Gold is sold today according to troy ounces. At the time of this writing (June 2010), the price of gold is about $1,289 per troy ounce. So in today's American dollar, that would put the value of the lamp stand at about $1,546,800. Well over 1.5 million dollars!

In Exodus 25:40 God tells Moses:

> See that you make *them* after the pattern for them, which was shown to you on the mountain.

Rashi, the famous Jewish commentator, makes the humorous (to us) comment that Moses was so confused by the instructions for making the menorah, that God had to show him a "fiery vision" of it.

Historical Significance

The lamp stand was used to provide light in the Holy Place so that it would never be dark. The Holy Place was illuminated either by daylight coming in through the entrance way of the Tabernacle, or by the light from the lamp stand. Historically, there are some very significant associations with the lamp stand, particularly between God and light. In the Bible, we see that God is light. Daniel 2:22 says:

> It is He **[speaking of God]** who reveals the profound and hidden things; He knows what is in the darkness, and the light dwells with Him.

We pick up this thought in Psalm 104:1-2:

> Bless the LORD, O my soul! O LORD my God, You are very great; You are clothed with splendor and majesty, covering Yourself with LIGHT as with a cloak, stretching out heaven like a *tent* curtain.

We also have the same association in the New Covenant in 1 John 1:5:

> This is the message we have heard from Him and announce to you, that God is Light, and in Him there is no darkness at all.

In scripture darkness is a symbol of sin, ignorance, error, and wickedness. There is no darkness associated with God. Note Proverbs 2:12-13:

> To deliver you from the way of evil, from the man who speaks perverse things; from those who leave the paths of righteousness to walk in the ways of darkness...

The way of evil is the way of darkness. The man who speaks perversely is the man who speaks dark things while walking down the way of darkness. If you leave uprightness and righteousness, Proverbs 4:19 very clearly states:

> The way of the wicked is like darkness; they do not know over what they stumble.

The wicked stumble in the dark trying to find their way. They do the best they can, but they constantly fall on their faces because they do not know the right way, the smooth way. They have no light so they cannot see the stones that cause them to stumble.

In contrast to this, there is no darkness in the Holy Place. The picture here is that there is no sin, no ignorance, no error, and no wickedness in the presence of God or in His character. God is light. In Him there is no darkness at all. This was the message of the lamp stand to ancient Israel.

Messianic Significance

The Messianic significance is just as clear. Jesus is the Light of the world. John 8:12 states:

> Then Jesus again spoke to them, saying, "I am the Light of the world; he who follows Me will not walk in the darkness, but will have the Light of life."

Rather than being the man in Proverbs 4:19 who is wicked and stumbling around not knowing where to go, Jesus says, *Walk with me, and I will provide you with Light; you will not have to stumble around in the dark wickedness of this world.*

Let us look also at John 9:5. Jesus says to the disciples:

> While I am in the world, I am the Light of the world.

Again there is no darkness if we walk with Him. He provides light for our path.

A very important theme in the book of John is the conflict between light and darkness. We are just touching on a few verses that deal with that theme. In John 12:46, Jesus said:

> I have come as Light into the world, so that everyone who believes in Me will not remain in darkness.

Without Jesus, we are stuck in darkness. That is the state of this world. We need the Messiah. We need Jesus to provide Light for us.

In Revelation 21:22-23, John is speaking of the eternal Jerusalem, which is the new Jerusalem, the Jerusalem of the eternal state:

> I saw no temple in it, for the Lord God the Almighty and the Lamb are its temple. And the city has no need of the sun or of the moon to shine on it, for the glory of God has illumined it, and its lamp *is* the Lamb.

According to scripture, there were to be four Temples constructed after the Tabernacle: the first Temple to be built by Solomon, the second Temple to be built by Zerubbabel, the third Temple to be built for the Tribulation, and, finally, the Messianic Temple. [The third and the fourth Temples have yet to be built.] After that, during the eternal state, there will not be a need for a Temple anymore because the Lamb will be the Temple at that time. The lamp of the new Jerusalem is also going to be the Lamb.

The lamp stand proclaims the Messiahship of *Yeshua*, Jesus. The lamp stand proclaims that there is no sin, no error, no ignorance or wickedness in the person of Jesus at all, and He is our Savior.

Application

And it gets even better! The scripture teaches that the believers, all of us who have placed our faith in Jesus, are lights as well. We get this teaching from Matthew 5:14-16 where Jesus tells the believers:

> You are the light of the world. A city set on a hill cannot be hidden; nor does *anyone* light a lamp and put it under a basket, but on a lamp stand, and it gives light to all who are in the house. Let your light shine before men in such a way that they may see your good works, and glorify your Father who is in heaven.

6. TABLE OF SHOWBREAD AND LAMP STAND

We are to be a light. There is supposed to be no sin, error, ignorance, or wickedness in our lives. When these qualities mark our character, we stand out from the world around us. We live righteously. Paul brings out this idea as he speaks to the men in Ephesians 5:8-9:

> For you were formerly darkness, but now you are Light in the Lord; walk as children of Light (for the fruit of the Light *consists* in all goodness and righteousness and truth.)

Let's ask ourselves, "Is my light shining before men? Do men see my good deeds and praise God our Father? Is my lifestyle righteous, making me stand out in the midst of our society? Am I living as a child of the Light, expressing goodness and righteousness and truth through my life? Or am I living as a child of the darkness and finding myself embroiled in error and ignorance and wickedness? I need to turn from error and ignorance and wickedness of this world and live for goodness and righteousness and truth."

One final application: There are many associations with lamp stands in scripture. One key association is with guidance.

Look at Psalm 119:105:

> Your word is a lamp to my feet and a light to my path.

If we are walking around in a dark world, we need a source of light. We need a lamp stand. The Word of God acts as a lamp and a light for the path that we walk.

Turn back to Psalm 18:28 for another very important application to our lives:

> For You light my lamp; the Lord my God illumines my darkness.

If we need wisdom, if we do not know where to go and what to do in this dark world, the Lord Himself will illuminate the way for us. We need to turn to Him and look to Him for the guidance we need to get through this world.

The writer of Proverbs 6:23 says:

> For the commandment is a lamp and the teaching is light;
> and reproofs for discipline are the way of life.

Looking into the Word of God and obeying Him will help us walk in the light so that we do not stumble in the dark. Are we looking into the Word of God for guidance in this dark world, or are we being deceived by looking to the world, or worse yet, trusting ourselves? This means we have to study the Word of God and know what it says, know what it means. But then we have to move on and use the Word of God in our lives on a daily basis to learn to distinguish between good and evil. Then we can walk down a path that is brightly illuminated for us.

7. TABERNACLE TENT

CURTAINS AND FRAMES

Exodus 25 focused on the inside of the Tabernacle tent. We looked at the Ark of the Covenant, the Table of Showbread and the lamp stand. Now we go on to Chapter 26 to see the surrounding tent itself.

We will begin in Exodus 26:1-6 with the description of the inner curtains. Do you notice a pattern here? We are starting from the inside, from the most significant part of the Tabernacle, and we are moving out. The most important part of the Tabernacle is the Holy of Holies that contained of Ark of the Covenant. Then we moved out into the Holy Place and looked at the Table of Showbread and the lamp stand. Now we are going to look at the covering for all of this.

Inner Curtains

Let's look at the inner curtains of the Tabernacle proper described in Exodus 26:1:

> Moreover you shall make the tabernacle with ten curtains of fine twisted linen and blue and purple and scarlet *material*; you shall make them with cherubim, the work of a skillful workman.

In verse 1, we see why God had the linen and yarn collected from Israel. Ten curtains are to be made from the highest quality linen and yarn that was available. In other words, the Tabernacle was made from materials fit for a king. The curtains were to have representations of the *cherubim* embroidered into them. This work in cloth was to be done by a skillful workman. Again the point is made that when we voluntarily give God our best, we do the very finest job we can. We do not present Him sloppy offerings, and we do not serve Him in a casual manner. We give Him our best! Now we must not get off balance. We must remember that we may not have the greatest skills in the world, but we do a good job for Him with the skills that we do possess.

Exodus 26:2 says:

> The length of each curtain shall be twenty-eight cubits, and the width of each curtain four cubits; all the curtains shall have the same measurements.

Thus the ten curtains are to be forty-two feet long and six feet wide.

Exodus 26:3 reads:

> Five curtains shall be joined to one another, and the other five curtains shall be joined to one another.

They were apparently sewn together in groups of five. This formed two larger curtains, forty-two feet long and thirty feet wide.

Exodus 26:4-6 tells us:

> You shall make loops of blue on the edge of the outermost curtain in the first set, and likewise you shall make them on the edge of the curtain that is outermost in the second set. You shall make fifty loops in the one curtain, and you shall make fifty loops on the edge of the curtain that is in the second set; the loops shall be opposite each other. You shall make fifty clasps of gold, and join the curtains to one another with the clasps so that the tabernacle will be a unit.

The two larger curtains were joined in the middle using these fifty sets of clasps and loops. A final, single curtain would have been created. That final, single curtain would be forty-two feet wide and sixty feet long. The reason for constructing the curtain of two main pieces was probably portability. They were apparently taken apart at that middle seam where the loops were located and then folded and transported.

There is a key word to note in this section. It is at the end of verse 6, where it says that the Tabernacle will be a unit.

The word "unit" is *echad* in Hebrew. It is the very same word that is used to describe God in the *Shema* in Deuteronomy 6:4. The word *echad* stresses compound unity. It is one thing made up of a number of components. The Tabernacle is made up of ten curtains, one hundred gold loops, and fifty gold clasps, and they are all joined together to become *echad*, a unit, a compound unity.

The significance is emphasized through the usage of *echad* in the *Shema* in Deuteronomy 6:4. Here it is not the Tabernacle that is being described; rather, God is being described as one: *Shema Yisrael Adonai Eloheynu Adonai Echad,* or in English:

Hear, O Israel! The LORD is our God, the LORD is one!

The usage of *echad* to describe God as one in the *Shema* hints at a very, very important theological truth. It opens the door to the doctrine of the triune nature of God.

Please note that the use of the word in Deuteronomy 6:4 does not prove plurality in the Godhead. Do not use Deuteronomy 6:4 to prove to someone that God is triune in nature. However, it does open the door to the truth that God is complex. God is a complex, compound unity. Of course, we get the full revelation from the New Testament that the God of Israel is one God made up of three distinguishable persons.

This truth is most explicitly stated in the New Covenant, Matthew 28:19. It is also revealed very strongly in the Hebrew Scriptures. Turn to Isaiah 48:16. Here God is speaking:

> Come near to Me, listen to this: From the first I have not spoken in secret, from the time it took place, I was there. And now the Lord GOD has sent Me, and His Spirit.

The individual who is speaking says He is from eternity past, from the time it took place, from the time matter existed, from the time creation existed, and He says, "I was there." This individual is unlimited by space and time, but this individual says the Lord GOD has sent Me and His Spirit. So this individual who is unlimited by space and time has to be GOD. That is the only person who can be described in those terms, GOD Himself. This person says that the Lord GOD sent Him. Now we have two people identified as GOD, and He ends up with the words, *and His Spirit*. Now we have three people associated with the same concept. The Hebrew Scriptures do not clearly teach or explicitly state that GOD is triune in nature. However, we do see a strong indication of it in the book of Isaiah.

It is in Matthew 28:19 that we get the explicit statements that are totally consistent with the book of Isaiah. Jesus says:

> Go therefore and make disciples of all the nations, baptizing them in the name of the Father and the Son and the Holy Spirit.

Jesus clearly states that GOD is triune in nature. The same three people that were seen in Isaiah 48:16 are seen here in Matthew 28:19. The original speaker would be the Son. The Lord GOD who sent Him would be GOD the Father, and of course, the Spirit would be the Holy Spirit. So *echad* is a very, very important word at the beginning of chapter 26.

Outer Curtains

The curtains mentioned above were the inner coverings of the Tabernacle. These were beautiful curtains with *cherubim* embroidered into them in blue, purple and scarlet. Now we move to the outer coverings of the Tabernacle in Exodus 26:7-14. We will start with verse 7:

> Then you shall make curtains of goats' *hair* for a tent over the tabernacle; you shall make eleven curtains in all.

This verse describes the coarse, black, goat hair coverings for the Tabernacle. Notice that this covering is called the tent for the Tabernacle. The word used in Hebrew is *ohel*. It means "tent." The word *ohel* emphasizes the temporary nature of this structure. It was designed to be portable. It was not designed to last forever. It would be replaced by a more permanent structure, the Temple itself. This goat hair covering was part of the protective outer layers of the Tabernacle. The Tabernacle itself was technically the structure within or under this tent. The tent or outer covering protected the Tabernacle from rain, sun, and dust; however, the linen inside is the Tabernacle proper.

Exodus 26:8-13 continues:

> The length of each curtain *shall be* thirty cubits, and the width of each curtain four cubits; the eleven curtains shall have the same measurements. You shall join five curtains by themselves and the *other* six curtains by themselves, and you shall double over the sixth curtain at the front of the tent. You shall make fifty loops on the edge of the curtain that is outermost in the *first* set, and fifty loops on the edge of the curtain *that is outermost in* the second set. You shall make fifty clasps of bronze, and you shall put the clasps into the loops and join the tent together so that it will

be a unit. The overlapping part that is left over in the curtains of the tent, the half curtain that is left over, shall lap over the back of the tabernacle. The cubit on one side and the cubit on the other, of what is left over in the length of the curtains of the tent, shall lap over the sides of the tabernacle on one side and on the other, to cover it.

These goat hair panels were forty-five feet long and six feet wide. Like the linen inner covering of the Tabernacle, they were sewn together into two larger sub-units. One sub-unit was five panels wide, forty-five feet by thirty feet, and the other sub unit was six panels wide, forty-five feet by thirty-six feet.

Again, like the inner coverings, the two large outer panels were joined into one unit through a series of one hundred loops and fifty bronze clasps. So the final size of the tent would be forty-five feet wide and sixty-six feet long.

This tent, being longer and wider than the inner Tabernacle curtains, effectively covered the Tabernacle. However, commentators are unsure as to exactly how the tent covered the Tabernacle. Some think it was a flat-roofed arrangement, and others think it was a peaked arrangement. That is why you will see drawings of both when you view pictures of the Tabernacle.

One drawback of a flattop design is that it serves very poorly in rainy weather. Flattop tents usually droop in the center and can get a huge pocket of water which is very difficult to drain. While the Sinai Peninsula is quite a bit drier than many places on earth, when it does rain there, it is quite a heavy rain. And, now and again, snow can fall. One commentator, James Strong, in his book *Tabernacle of Israel* writes:

The rainfall during the showers in the winter on the Sinai Peninsula is often prodigious, and snow occasionally falls to the depth of several inches in the valleys around Mount Sinai.

Apparently in March 1874, Strong and his party were overtaken at Mount Sinai by a snowstorm of such severity as to compel them to take refuge in the convent there for several days. So there you have it from a man who has been there.

If the Tabernacle trekked around the Sinai Peninsula for some forty years, there certainly was the possibility of having to endure a wide range of weather conditions—unless, of course, God miraculously shielded the Tabernacle from the weather. However, that does not seem to be the case. It appears that God had these protective layers constructed in order to shield the Tabernacle from rain, perhaps from snow, from wind, and from dust.

Of course, there is a third option for the design of the Tabernacle and its covering which would be a combination of both. Perhaps the inner covering was flat and topped with the outer coverings that were peaked.

Now let us move on to Exodus 26:14:

> You shall make a covering for the tent of rams' skins dyed red and a covering of porpoise skins above.

In this verse, two other durable, weather-resistant layers of the tent are described. Some think they went under and others think they went over the goat hair layer. We think these went on top of the goat hair curtains themselves. The terminology supports this position because these layers are called a covering. The goat hair was called a curtain. The position in the text following the description of the curtains also indicates that they went over the top of the goat hair curtain. Remember, we are moving from the interior to the exterior of the structure. As these coverings are not described in detail, it implies that their construction and their dimensions were identical to the goat hair layer.

Let us summarize what we have just read. First of all, we have seen one inner, linen layer that comprised the Tabernacle itself, and it was blue, purple and scarlet with *cherubim* embroidered into the linen. This inner, linen layer is the Tabernacle itself, the Tabernacle proper. Then there is an outer layer called a tent and two more outer layers called the covering for the tent. The tent and the outer layers are all protective of the Tabernacle itself.

Frames

In Exodus 15-25, we learn about the frames that supported the tent. Exodus 26:15-17:

> Then you shall make the boards for the tabernacle of acacia wood, standing upright. Ten cubits *shall be* the length of each board and one and a half cubits the width of each board. *There shall be* two tenons for each board, fitted to one another; thus you shall do for all the boards of the tabernacle.

Some of the commentators view these as solid boards. You will notice that we call them frames. The word board is used in the American Standard Version, the New American Standard Version, and the King James Version. The New International Version (NIV) uses the word frames. We think the NIV is the most accurate in this particular case. The Hebrew word is *qeresh*. In the Encyclopedia Judaica, we read this comment about a *qeresh*:

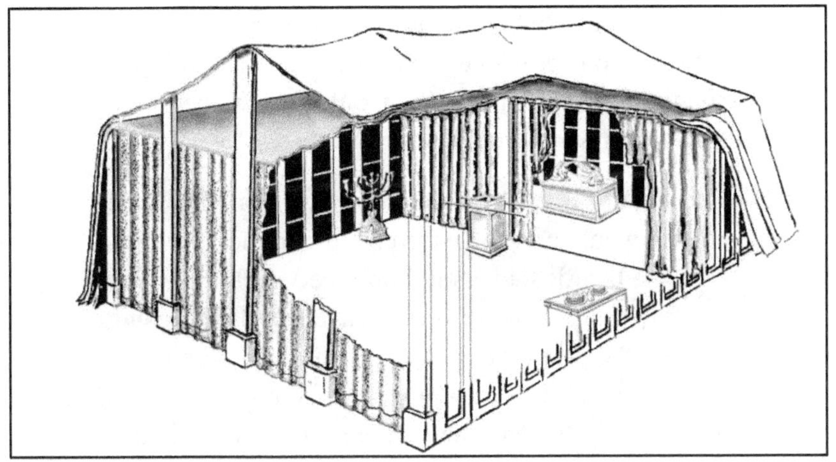

Figure 8. The Tent of Meeting

Most exegetes now accept the view of A. R. S. Kennedy, that qeresh denotes a light open frame, consisting of two side arms joined together at the top, the middle and the foot by cross rungs with two tenons projecting below.

That is probably the best description of these frames. (See Figure 8 for an artistic conception of the frames.). The understanding that the walls of the Tabernacle were really frames has four distinct advantages over viewing them as boards.

1)   The walls of the Tabernacle would be more portable and much lighter in weight than solid boards. Remember, these had to be trekked around the Sinai Peninsula.

2)   Less material would be used in the making of these wooden frames, and less gold would be needed to overlay them.

3) The frames would also provide better ventilation. Unless God provided His own supernatural air-conditioning system, frames would provide better air flow than boards would.

4) The beautiful embroidered *cherubim* on the linen curtain would be visible through the frames, whereas with the boards they would only be visible overhead if the priests were to look heavenward. By using frames, the priest would see the blue, the purple, the scarlet, and the *cherubim* through each frame immediately when they entered the Holy Place. Also, when the High Priest entered the Holy of Holies, they would see themselves surrounded by depictions of God's throne attendants, the *cherubim*. It would be as though they were actually in the heavenly Tabernacle itself surrounded by the magnificent glory of that true Tabernacle in the heavenly realm.

These frames formed the walls of the Tabernacle. The dimensions of the frames are fifteen feet high, two-feet-three inches wide (based on what we read in Exodus 26:16). At the bottom, two projections would protrude from the base of each frame. They were probably just extensions of the side beams. These projections fit into silver bases, two for each frame, and these bases then acted as a foundation for the structure

As we move into lesson eight of our study, we will learn just how these frames were utilized in the Tabernacle construction.

8. MORE CONSTRUCTION AND LOGISTICS

FRAMES, VEIL, AND FURNITURE PLACEMENT

More About Frames

Let's continue reading about the frames in Exodus 26:18-25:

> You shall make the boards for the tabernacle: twenty boards for the south side. You shall make forty sockets of silver under the twenty boards, two sockets under one board for its two tenons and two sockets under another board for its two tenons; for the second side of the tabernacle, on the north side, twenty boards, their forty sockets of silver; two sockets under one board and two sockets under another board. For the rear of the tabernacle, to the west, you shall make six boards. You shall make two boards for the corners of the tabernacle at the rear. They shall be double beneath and together they shall be complete to its top to the first ring; thus it shall be with both of them: they shall form the two corners. There shall be eight boards with their sockets of silver, sixteen sockets; two sockets under one board and two sockets under another board.

A cutaway drawing shows some possible details of how these boards were fit together in the Tabernacle (Figure 9).

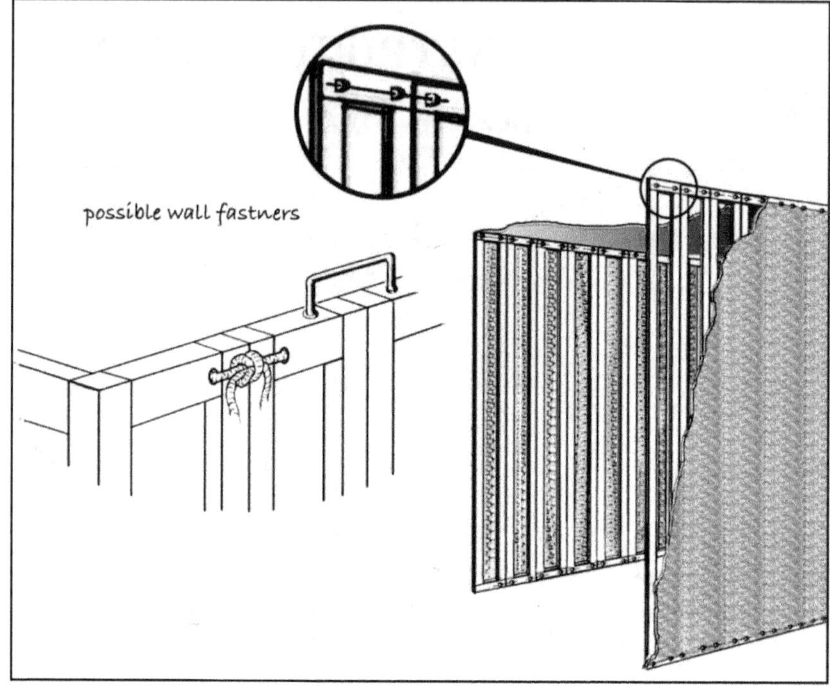

Figure 9. Tabernacle Wall Fasteners

The frames were positioned side by side. The Tabernacle was twenty frames long and six frames wide, making the Tabernacle fifteen feet wide and forty-five feet long. There were no frames across the east end, the front end of the structure, so it was three-sided with boards around the west and the north and the south, forming a U-shape.

Now we come to Exodus 26:26-29 and the crossbars:

> Then you shall make bars of acacia wood, five for the boards on one side of the tabernacle, and five bars for the boards on the other side of the tabernacle, and five bars for the boards of the side of the tabernacle for the rear *side* to the west. The middle bar in the center of the boards shall

> pass through from end to end. You shall overlay the boards
> with gold and make their rings of gold as holders for the
> bars; and you shall overlay the bars with gold.

Each of the three walls was reinforced by five horizontal bars attached by rings to the frames. The center bar was of one piece. The upper and lower bars were split at the middle, making two upper bars and two lower bars.

These wood frames and their bars were all overlaid with gold in keeping with preparing the dwelling place of the King. This was to be the King's chambers, the throne room, and the reception room. It was to be made from the very best that Israel had to offer: gold.

Exodus 26:30 is a very important verse:

> Then you shall erect the tabernacle according to its plan,
> which you have been shown in the mountain.

Verse 30 says to set up a Tabernacle according to the plan. The word *plan* is used here, not *pattern*. Previously the word used was *tavnit*. Here the word used is *mishpat*. *Mishpat* is a legal word. It means judgment in a judicial sense or a carefully considered decision. It is a much more personal word than the word used for pattern. This pattern that Moses is being commanded to follow is not some impersonal blueprint. The use of the word *mishpat* shows God's direct involvement in the design of the Tabernacle. The design is God's personal and carefully considered decision. So this word strongly emphasizes God's personal involvement in the design of the Tabernacle. *Tavnit* or *pattern* is an impersonal word identifying the specifications, the blueprint, the plans. But *mishpat* is a personal word that identifies the architect. The architect of the blueprint is God Himself. This word reinforces the importance of Moses following the pattern exactly, for it is the personal directive of the King of kings, who is personally interested that it is done right.

Veil

Exodus 26:31-33 tells about the veil of the Tabernacle:

> You shall make a veil of blue and purple and scarlet *material* and fine twisted linen; it shall be made with cherubim, the work of a skillful workman. You shall hang it on four pillars of acacia overlaid with gold, their hooks *also being of* gold, on four sockets of silver. You shall hang up the veil under the clasps, and shall bring in the ark of the testimony there within the veil; and the veil shall serve for you as a partition between the holy place and the holy of holies.

We now see that the Tabernacle is divided into two rooms. It is divided into the Holy Place, the *qodesh,* the outer room; and the Holy of Holies, the *qodesh haqodashim,* the inner room.

The means for dividing the Tabernacle into two rooms is a veil. This curtain or veil is suspended on four posts across the width of the room. No dimensions are given in the text for the placement of the veil. Does it go near the front, does it go near the back, or does it go in the middle? Nothing is said. The positioning of the veil must be deduced by comparing it to the floor plans of Solomon's Temple. Since it was a permanent version of the portable Tabernacle, it's reasonable to look at Solomon's Temple to deduce where the veil was located.

I Kings 6:16-17 states that Solomon's Temple was divided in the ratio of 2 to 1. That would make the Holy of Holies in Solomon's Temple a perfect cube that extended one-third the length of the building.

This same pattern was followed in later Temples as well. If we follow that pattern, then, the veil was placed fifteen feet from the west end of the Tabernacle. This partitioned off the Holy of Holies

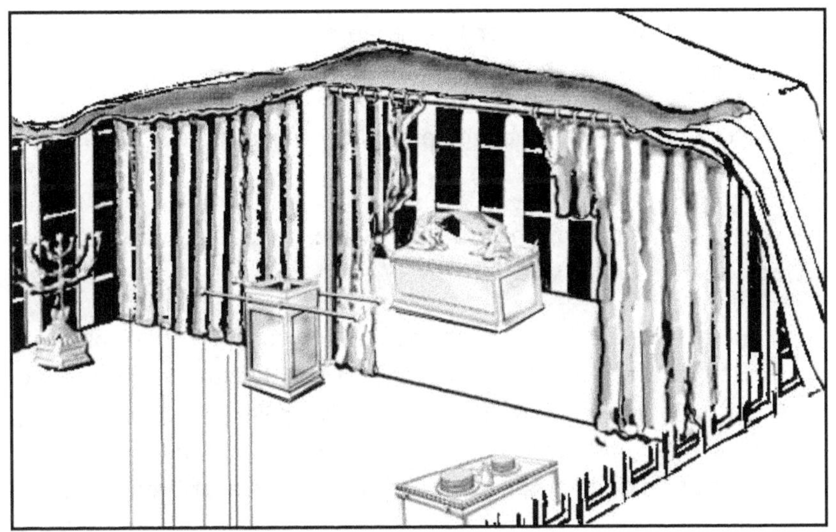

Figure 10. Tabernacle Rooms and Furnishings

into a small, inner room fifteen feet in length, in height, and in width. The Ark of the Covenant was then placed in the Holy of Holies (see Figure 10). As we have previously seen, the veil was made from blue, purple, and scarlet yarn; it was made from the highest quality cloth available, and it was decorated with the most skillful embroidery that Israel had to offer. It was worthy of being part of the King's dwelling place.

Placement of the Furniture

We now come to the placement of the furniture in Exodus 26:34-35:

> And you shall put the mercy seat on the ark of the testimony in the Holy of Holies. (The lid is placed upon the Ark of the Covenant.) You shall set the table outside the veil, (that is in the holy place), and the lamp stand opposite

the table on the side of the tabernacle toward the south; and you shall put the table on the north side.

The table and the lamp stand are placed on opposite sides of the Holy Place.

As we continue moving toward the outside, we come to the entrance of the Tabernacle in Exodus 26:36-37:

You shall make a screen for the doorway of the tent of blue and purple and scarlet *material* and fine twisted linen, the work of a weaver. You shall make five pillars of acacia for the screen and overlay them with gold, their hooks *also being of* gold; and you shall cast five sockets of bronze for them.

Now we take a look at the entrance curtain to the Tabernacle. Again, the entrance curtain is made from the best material available. This entrance curtain is luxurious, costly, and it speaks of the magnificence of the royalty within.

The entrance curtain was hung on posts overlaid with gold. The only difference between these posts and all the others is that these are set in foundations of bronze. This is a less valuable material. Do you notice a pattern here? As we begin to move away from the King's dwelling chambers, the materials used become less and less valuable. These bronze bases are the first common metals to be used in the construction of the Tabernacle. Notice also, the Tabernacle linen coverings were put together with clasps of gold, but the protective outer coverings were made of clasps of bronze. The same thing is happening here. As we move to the outside, the bases are made of bronze instead of silver.

HISTORICAL SIGNIFICANCE OF THE TABERNACLE

What is the historical significance of the Tabernacle? First of all, the Tabernacle was the dwelling place of the King of Israel. The Holy of Holies is the throne room, and the Holy Place is the reception room of the palace. As we draw nearer and nearer to the throne room, we experience the increasing sanctity and holiness of the royal person.

The entrance curtain signified separation and limited access. Only Priests could enter into the Holy Place. Hebrews 9:6-7 tells us:

> Now when these things have been so prepared, the priests are continually entering the outer tabernacle performing the divine worship, but into the second, only the high priest *enters* once a year, not without *taking* blood, which he offers for himself and for the sins of the people committed in ignorance.

Here again, we see that repeated; only the Priests could come into the Holy Place. The ordinary Israelite could not, so the entrance curtain separated the Priests from the rest of Israel. Only a Levite could enter that outer room of the Tabernacle. Entrance to the King is limited. He is separated, he is special, and he is sanctified.

Now what about the veil? Just as the entrance curtain historically spoke of separation, the veil signifies separation and limited access into the Holy of Holies. Only the High Priest was permitted into the Holy of Holies, and that access was allowed on only one day per year, Yom Kippur.

That whole issue of separation is repeated in Leviticus 16:2. Only one man, from one family, from one tribe, from one nation out of the entire world was ever able to enter into the very presence of God, and that was for only one day out of the year. There was a separation between God and man, and very, very limited access to God. This teaches us that God is not a trivial being Whom we can take for granted.

MESSIANIC SIGNIFICANCE

As we come to the Messianic significance of all this, we need to begin by discussing the veil. For this, we turn to Matthew 27:50-51. Jesus is now on the cross. He is suffering on the cross for you and me. He is about to die:

> And Jesus cried out again with a loud voice, and yielded up His spirit. **[That is the moment of his physical death.]** And behold, the veil of the temple was torn in two from top to bottom; and the earth shook and the rocks were split.

It was the veil in Herod's Temple that was split from top to bottom the moment the Messiah died. Here is a description of that veil, taken from the *Mishna, Shekalim* 8:4-5. Rabban Simon Ben Gamliel says in the name of Rabbi Shimon:

> The veil was one hand breadth thick and was woven on a loom having 72 rods. And over each rod were 24 threads. Its length was 40 cubits. Its breadth was 20 cubits. It was made by 82 young girls and they used to make two in every year. And 300 priests immersed it.

This section from the *Mishna* tells us that the veil in Herod's Temple was approximately four inches thick, sixty feet long and thirty feet wide. In other words, the veil in Herod's Temple was not some flimsy bed sheet or piece of linen. It was not something you could tear up with your bare hands and throw in your rag bag. The veil in Herod's Temple was thick and strong, heavy and massive. This is what God tore from top to bottom. With the death of Jesus, the thick, heavy, strong, massive separation that existed between God and man was ended. The Temple veil was ripped in two, and therefore, all who place their faith in Jesus now have access to God because that massive, strong, thick, barrier has been opened and taken out of our way.

Hebrews 10:19-20 tells us:

> Therefore, brethren, since we have confidence to enter the holy place by the blood of Jesus, by a new and living way, which He inaugurated for us through the veil, that is, His flesh...

All who personally receive Jesus as their Savior and Messiah gain access to God. The Tabernacle veil pictured His flesh, which was torn in death and suffering for you and me. Because the death of Jesus ended the separation between God and man, the veil is a symbol of His body. We have a new and living way inaugurated for us through the veil.

The second point of Messianic significance deals with the Tabernacle as it is associated with Jesus' body, also a Tabernacle. In John 1:14 we read:

> And the Word became flesh, and dwelt among us, and we saw his glory, glory as of the only begotten from the Father, full of grace and truth.

Remember, that word *dwelt* is a Grecianized version of the Hebrew word *Shekinah* or Tabernacle: Jesus *tabernacled* among us.

In John 2:18, as Jesus cleanses Herod's Temple we learn:

> The Jews then said to Him, "What sign do You show us as your authority for doing these things?"

John 2:19-22 tells us how Jesus responded:

> Jesus answered them, "Destroy this temple, and in three days I will raise it up." The Jews then said, "It took forty-six years to build this temple, and will You raise it up in three days?" But He was speaking of the temple of His body. So when He was raised from the dead, His disciples remembered that He said this; and they believed the Scripture and the word which Jesus had spoken.

Jesus tells the Jews that his body is a temple and will be raised in three days.

The Tabernacle was where God dwelt with man. In the book of Exodus, God resided in a tent. He lived and dwelled, so to speak, in the midst of Israel. Jesus, in the same way as God "put on" or dwelled in a tent, put on a human body. God dwelt among the Israelites in the person of Jesus.

APPLICATION

What can all this mean to us today? Quite significantly, when you become a believer in the Messiah, your body then becomes a temple of God.

Paul emphasizes this to the Corinthians, urging them to flee immorality and not to participate in sins against their own physical body. He goes on to say in 1 Corinthians 6:19-20:

> Or do you not know that your body is a temple of the Holy Spirit who is in you, whom you have from God, and that you are not your own? For you have been bought with a price: therefore glorify God in your body.

God dwells in you, and God dwells in me, in the presence of the Holy Spirit, in the presence of the *Ruach HaQodesh*. He dwells in you, and He dwells in me, in the same way that He dwelled in the Tabernacle.

The point is this. How do you treat your body? Do you treat it with the same care that you would treat the Tabernacle? Or do you treat it sloppily, carelessly? Do you honor God in your body? Or do you dishonor God? That is the context of 1 Corinthians 6:12-18. Verses 12-18 deals with moral laxity and moral sloppiness. Paul encourages us to honor God and use our bodies properly, in a righteous way.

Now let's turn our thoughts to the entrance of the Tabernacle. As previously mentioned, only Priests were allowed into God's dwelling place. Only Priests could pass through the separation caused by the curtain. But did you know that when you become a believer in Jesus, you also become a Priest? Revelation 5:9 tells us:

> And they sang a new song, saying, "Worthy are You to take the book and to break its seals; for You were slain, and purchased for God with your blood *men* from every tribe and tongue and people and nation.

The reference to every tribe and tongue and people and nation is a reference to the church made up of believers from all over the world. And they have been made for what? Revelation 5:10 explains:

> You have made them *to be* a kingdom and priests to our God; and they will reign upon the earth.

We are Priests, and we will administer the divine services as we also co-reign with Jesus during the Messianic Kingdom. Revelation 20:6 repeats this:

> Blessed and holy is the one who has a part in the first resurrection; over these the second death has no power, but they will be priests of God and of Christ and will reign with Him for a thousand years.

Believers are Priests, people from all over the world who have been set aside to administer the divine services.

This is the question we now need to ask, "How am I living out on a practical, everyday basis in my everyday life the fact that I am a temple of the living God and the fact that I am a Priest of the living God? How do I care for my body? How do I care for God's temple?"

This study of Exodus 26 leads us to a call for righteous and holy living. We are no longer what we once were. You may have come from a very difficult background. You may be carrying around some very heavy emotional baggage that was heaped upon you by your family. For example, if you were born into a family where one or both of your parents were alcoholics, you might have a very low self image. But when you come to believe in Jesus the Messiah, when you yield to Him and His ways, He will raise you out of that pit (of whatever emotional baggage you might be carrying). You will no longer be what you once were. You will no longer be in darkness. You are no longer insignificant. You will now be in the light of the LORD. You will be living according to your new position, and with the LORD'S help, you are able to walk according to your new position. Remember, you are a temple and a Priest. You are no longer in darkness, despair, sin, error, and ignorance.

We implore you, if you are having trouble with your self-image and who you are, do not get your self-image from the world or from worldly psychology that says "I'm okay, you're okay." That is very shallow compared to what the Bible tells us. Please get your self-image from the truth of scripture and how God views you.

From the truth of scripture, we learn that we are Priests and a temple of the living God. We are the temple of the God of the universe. We are Priests who serve the ever-living, omniscient God. We need to walk in the light of that revelation and choose to believe it. It is hard if you come from a family that is dysfunctional. It is hard to believe that you can be worth something, but you must choose to believe that in the Messiah, you become more precious than gold. God would not lie to you.

Do not base the truth on your emotions. Truth is truth no matter what your feelings tell you. Accepting the LORD into your life is based on your will, not your emotions. The feelings will follow. What the Bible says is true. Affirm that truth and with the LORD'S help, live the truth out on a day-to-day basis.

There are many things that happen when you accept the LORD into your heart, but from these particular verses, I pray you'll rejoice that we are God's temple, and we are Priests of the living God.

9. BRONZE ALTAR

BRONZE ALTAR DESCRIPTION

Exodus 27:1-2 describes the altar:

> And you shall make the altar of acacia wood, five cubits long and five cubits wide; the altar shall be square, and its height shall be three cubits. You shall make its horns on its four corners; its horns shall be of one piece with it, and you shall overlay it with bronze.

As we look at the dimensions of the altar, we find that Israel is to construct a box four-feet-six inches high and about seven-feet-six inches along the side (see Figure 11).

Horns

Specifically mentioned in verse 2 are the horns of the altar. Moses is to make horns on its four corners. Now what in the world is God talking about? Horns are a normal design feature of many altars in the Ancient Near East. They were triangular or square protrusions jutting up from the corners of the altar and symbolic of an animal's horn.

What was the importance of a horn? The horns on an animal were the focus of the beast's power. Therefore, they came to denote physical might and power.

For example, take a look at Deuteronomy 33:17. This is the blessing of the 12 tribes. Moses is blessing Joseph.

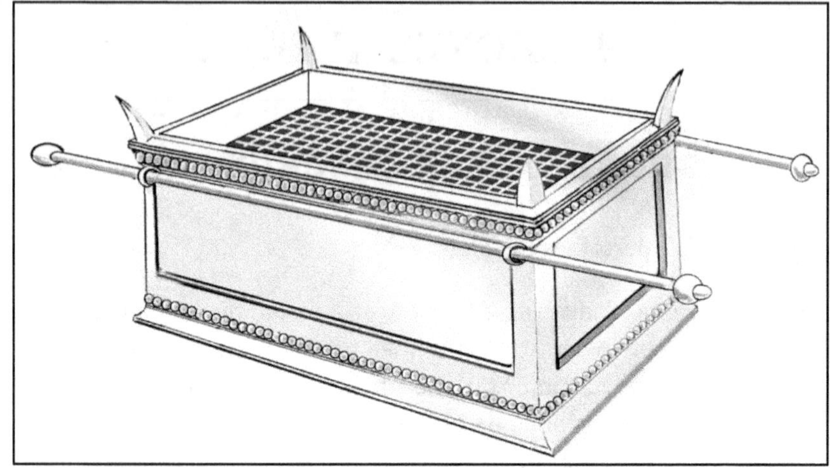

Figure 11. The Bronze Altar

As the firstborn of his ox, majesty is his, and his horns are the horns of the wild ox; with them he shall push the peoples, all at once, to the ends of the earth. And those are the ten thousands of Ephraim, and those are the thousands of Manasseh.

As Jacob blesses Joseph's tribe, he blesses them with physical might and power. That was a significance of horns in general. But horns on altars focused on the symbolic presence and power of God.

David writes a psalm in 2 Samuel 22. He writes about God; he extols God, and in verse 3 he declares,

My God, my rock, in whom I take refuge, my shield and the horn of my salvation, my stronghold and my refuge; my savior, You save me from violence.

When David wants to praise God and to emphasize God's mighty power in saving him, he describes God as the horn of his salvation, his strength and source.

Horns on the altar were also a place of refuge. We see this in 1 Kings 1:49-50. Adonijah, one of the sons of David, is trying to usurp the throne from the new king, Solomon. He has not been chosen to be the next king, but he is trying to become king anyway. He has put in place a plan for succession that he thinks has been successful, so he is celebrating. We come to verse 49 where Adonijah gets the word that King Solomon has learned of his plan to usurp the throne.

> Then all the guests of Adonijah were terrified, and they arose and each went on his own way.

The guests immediately realized that their lives would be in danger if Solomon found out that they had been supporting Adonijah. Adonijah's response is recorded in 1 Kings 1:50:

> And Adonijah was afraid of Solomon, and he arose, went and took hold of the horns of the altar.

Why did he do that? Refugees seeking asylum seized the altar horns. He was safe as long as he was in that position. It was a place of refuge.

The altar was overlaid with bronze, and bronze is associated with judgment. So this was also a place of judgment.

Let us summarize what we have learned about the altar to this point. Two seemingly contradictory ideas meet here. The altar is the place of God's presence, the place of His power, and the place of His judgment. But the altar can also be the place of His mercy and of refuge.

Utensils

In Exodus 27:3 we read:

> You shall make its pails for removing its ashes, and its shovels and its basins and its forks and its firepans; you shall make all its utensils of bronze.

The sacrifices of the Mosaic sacrificial system were burned on this altar. Therefore, this verse is a summary verse encompassing all the utensils needed to manage fires, ashes, and burnt sacrifices. All are made of bronze. All were associated with judgment.

This altar is also significantly linked with fire since the sacrifices were burned here, and fire is another symbol of judgment. For example, Isaiah 66:15-16 says:

> For behold, the Lord will come in fire And His chariots like the whirlwind, To render His anger with fury, And His rebuke with flames of fire. For the Lord will execute judgment by fire And by His sword on all flesh, And those slain by the Lord will be many.

Grate

God takes two verses to describe this grating for us in Exodus 27:4-5:

> You shall make for it a grating of network of bronze, and on the net you shall make four bronze rings at its four corners. You shall put it beneath, under the ledge of the altar, so that the net will reach halfway up the altar.

The instructions for this grating are a little vague. Consequently, there are varying opinions regarding the position of the grating. Some feel that it would sit on the top of the altar and others believe it would be located in the middle of the altar. Some see it sliding through a slot in the side of the altar, others, sliding up from the bottom of the altar. There are quite a number of options for how the grating was related to the altar. But it probably sat halfway up the inside of the altar.

Some also think that this grating was a support for a ledge that protruded from the altar. According to Jewish tradition, there was a ledge there, and it was one cubit or eighteen inches wide; the Priests stood on it to manage the burning sacrifices more efficiently.

Poles

Exodus 27:6-7 states:

> You shall make poles for the altar, poles of acacia wood, and overlay them with bronze. Its poles shall be inserted into the rings, so that the poles shall be on the two sides of the altar when it is carried.

Consistent with all the other articles of the Tabernacle, this altar was designed to be portable. We see that the carrying poles were part of the design. They are also covered with bronze reminding us of judgment.

Hollow

In verse 8, we come to a very significant verse regarding the placement of the altar. God's charge is:

> You shall make it hollow with planks; as it was shown you in the mountain, so they shall make *it*.

Most likely an earthen mound was raised up in the middle of the Tabernacle compound, and the altar was placed over that pile of earth. The four walls surrounded it, and the earth mound probably then supported the grate and helped to bear the weight of the heavy sacrifices. It may have helped withstand the wear caused by the heavy wood and the heat of the fire.

Then we come to the charge. The altar was also to be made hollow so it was easy to carry from place to place. This charge once again emphasizes the care and the accuracy that was to be used in the construction of all the aspects of the Tabernacle. Everything was to be accurately and responsibly constructed exactly according to God's design.

HISTORICAL SIGNIFICANCE

There are four points to consider.

First: To summarize, the horns on the altar focused on the symbolic presence and power of God in judgment.

Second: We need to remember that horns on the altar were also a place of refuge, a place where a refugee asked for mercy from judgment.

Third: However, we need to recall that atonement is by means of blood. There were animals sacrificed and burned upon this altar. The animal would be the sinner's substitute. The animal would be sacrificed near the altar, some of the blood would be placed on the horns of the altar, and the rest would be poured out at the base of the altar. So the altar was the place where the blood was spilled.

That term *spilling of the blood* or *the blood was spilt* is in many cases a euphemism, a more gentle way of describing a violent death.

We see a similar figure of speech used in the scriptures in other places.

For example, the writer of Proverbs 6:16-17 states:

> There are six things which the LORD hates, yes, seven which are an abomination to Him: Haughty eyes, a lying tongue, and hands that shed innocent blood.

When the proverb says *hands that shed innocent blood*, it refers to God despising hands that cause the violent death of an innocent person. Murder is despised by God.

We also know from Leviticus 17:11 that blood is a symbol of the life of a creature. God says that the life of the creature is in the blood. When the blood is gone from the creature, the life is gone.

There is great significance in these two symbols in relation to the altar, as we learn in Hebrews 9:22:

> And according to the Law, *one may* almost *say,* all things are cleansed with blood, and without shedding of blood there is no forgiveness.

An absolutely holy and righteous God does not tolerate sin. Sin causes hostility between God and the sinner. Remember the symbolism portrayed by the veil? That thick, massive, heavy veil was between the Holy of Holies and the Holy Place. It speaks of the hostility and the separation between God and man due to sin. Sin is an affront to God that must be dealt with. Yet God, in his infinite love, does not want to destroy the sinner. At the same time, that infinite love cries out for satisfaction. Reconciliation must occur, and the only possible solution is the death of the sinner. That is exactly what Romans 6:23 says, "The wages of sin is death."

Romans 6:23 speaks of both death and spiritual separation from God. Death in scripture is not "ceasing to exist." It is separation and the lack of relationship. When one dies physically, that person does not cease to exist, but he is no longer able to have a relationship with those in the land of the living. When one is spiritually dead, he has no ability to have a relationship with God. One finds himself separated from God on a spiritual plane, and then eventually, separated from man on a physical plane. So most truly, the wages of sin is death.

However, out of His great love, God is willing to provide a solution. God is willing to accept a substitute. A substitute can die in the place of the sinner. That is the good news. The bad news is our sin, which separates us from God. The altar is where the violent death of the substitute occurred. That is where the blood was spilled. This is the place of satisfaction; this is the place of atonement.

Can you see why the altar seemed to be symbolic of two contradictory themes? It was to be symbolic of judgment with the bronze, but it was also symbolic of mercy. It was a place of refuge, but judgment must also occur. The substitute must die, but mercy is also there because the sinner is then set free.

Fourth: We come to the fourth historical significance of the altar. The altar is where justification occurred. These are the steps. When the substitute dies, God's wrath against sin is appeased. Since God is satisfied, reconciliation occurs. When reconciliation occurs between the sinner and God, then God justifies the sinner.

What do we mean by the statement "God justifies the sinner?" Justification is a legal term that means to declare someone not guilty. If someone stood before a judge, and the judge heard the case and pronounced his verdict, "Not guilty," he would be justifying the person who stood before him. It is here that the declaration "Not guilty" was pronounced. The altar is where the substitute dies. The substitute is judged guilty and then experiences the penalty (death) for sin. The substitute is an animal. The animal is an innocent substitute even though the penalty for the guilt is being laid upon him. But the real sinner, the one who actually is guilty, is declared not guilty because the penalty has been dealt out on the substitute.

MESSIANIC SIGNIFICANCE

Jesus is the final and ultimate substitutionary sacrifice. Jesus offered Himself as the atoning sacrifice that satisfied God's wrath against sin and justifies us.

Hebrews 9:13 tells us:

> For if the blood of goats and bulls and the ashes of a heifer sprinkling those who have been defiled [serve to] sanctify [sinners] for the cleansing of the flesh...

The author is talking about the Mosaic system of sacrifice that began with the Tabernacle and continued on through the Temples. The Mosaic system is the lesser way, a shadow of the real thing to come.

In Hebrews 9:14-15, the author continues, talking about the real thing, the blood of Messiah:

> ...how much more will the blood of Christ **[we have moved from the lesser to the greater]**, who through the eternal Spirit offered Himself without blemish to God, cleanse your conscience **[not just cleansing of the flesh of dirt and blood, but internal cleansing]** from dead works to serve the living God? For this reason He is the mediator of a new covenant, so that, since a death has taken place for the redemption of the transgressions that were *committed* under the first covenant, those who have been called may receive the promise of the eternal inheritance.

Jesus' death provided the atoning sacrifice for us, and that is where we receive justification.

Romans 3:21-26 deals with this idea of justification:

> But now, apart from the Law **[the Mosaic Law]** *the* righteousness of God has been manifested, being witnessed by the Law and the Prophets, even *the* righteousness of God through faith in Jesus Christ for all those who believe; for there is no distinction; for all **[all people]** have sinned and fall short of the glory of God, being justified **[declared not guilty]** as a gift by His grace through the redemption which is in Christ Jesus; whom God displayed publicly as a propitiation in His blood through faith. *This was* to demonstrate His righteousness, because in the forbearance of God He passed over the sins previously committed; for the demonstration, *I say,* of His righteousness at the present time, so that He would be just and the justifier of the one who has faith in Jesus.

These verses show the anger of God and the offense God feels against sin. He needs to do what is right; all that is wrong needs to be righted. He must be just, but He balanced His love and His justice. Let us read Romans 3:26 again:

> For the demonstration, *I say,* of His righteousness at the present time, **[is so]** that He might be just and the justifier of the one who has faith in Jesus.

Do you see His mercy coming out? Being just focuses on God's wrath, and being the justifier focuses on His mercy. Remember how we saw the two concepts brought out in the altar? The altar was a place of judgment but also the place of refuge and mercy. The altar pictured what Paul describes.

Now, we need to bring out just one more point. Jesus is also the altar as well as the sacrifice. The author of Hebrews 13:10 says:

> We have an altar from which those who serve the tabernacle have no right to eat.

The author is using the Tabernacle as his picture. He says that the believer today has a different altar. It is not a physical altar.

He goes on to say in Hebrews 13:11-12:

> For the bodies of those animals whose blood is brought into the holy place by the high priest *as an offering* for sin, are burned outside the camp. Therefore Jesus also, that He might sanctify the people through His own blood, suffered outside the gate.

Do you see the parallels? The offering was burned outside the camp. There is a symbolic altar outside the camp. Those who identify with the camp have no right to fellowship at this altar. However, Jesus is associated with this symbolic altar because Jesus also went outside the camp. Let us read Hebrews 13:12 again:

> Therefore Jesus also, that He might sanctify the people through His own blood, suffered outside the gate.

Now what should be the response to that verse? Hebrews 13:13 urges us:

> So, let us go out to Him outside the camp, bearing His reproach.

Let us identify with Him. For here, inside the Jewish community, inside the Mosaic Law, inside the shadows, we do not have a lasting city. Inside the physical realm, nothing is permanent. Hebrews 13:14-15 adds:

> For here we do not have a lasting city, but we are seeking *the city* which is to come. Through Him then, let us continually offer up a sacrifice of praise to God, that is, the fruit of lips that give thanks to His name.

The author is saying if we choose to fellowship and identify with Jesus and His altar, we can continually offer up sacrifices to God without limitations. We do not offer up literal sacrifices on a physical altar; they are not needed at this time. Rather, we offer up the sacrifice of praise on this symbolic altar. Jesus is not only our sacrifice but he is our altar as well.

APPLICATION

In light of this lesson, ask yourself, "Is Jesus my atoning sacrifice?" If He is not, and you know that He is not, we beg you to please come to Him and receive the sacrifice that He made on your behalf.

Ask yourself as well, "Did Jesus die for me? Is God's wrath against my sins satisfied? Has God declared me not guilty?"

If you are not sure, or if your answer is no, then what are you going to do about it? "Will you come to Jesus and ask for forgiveness for your sins? Will you come to the altar and receive the sacrifice that He made for you?"

Here is another very, very important question we need to ask at this point. "Have I ever been afraid of losing my salvation?" Some branches of Christianity do teach this. They teach that you can be saved; but if you sin in a severe enough manner (and what constitutes a severe enough manner varies with different churches), you can lose your salvation and have to be "re-saved" all over again.

However, we do not believe that teaching. We believe the Bible very clearly teaches what is called eternal security. That means it is impossible to lose your salvation once you have established a relationship with God. Because we know many people struggle with the assurance of their salvation, we want to assure you that you cannot lose your salvation, because God has declared you "not guilty." You cannot find a judge any higher than Him. Being declared not guilty is a one-time event. When you have been declared not guilty, you are not guilty!

In addition to that, we want you to understand that salvation exists in three tenses; a past tense, a present tense, and a future tense.

The past tense could be described with this sentence. The believer **has been** saved from the guilt and penalty of sin. Some verses that would substantiate that statement are Luke 7:50, Ephesians 2:5-8, and 2 Timothy 1:8-9.

The second tense of salvation is the present tense. The believer **is being** saved from the power, the habit, and the dominion of sin. Verses to substantiate this thought are 1 Corinthians 1:18, 2 Corinthians 2:15, 2 Thessalonians 2:13, and Philippians 2:12-13.

We also have the future tense of salvation. The believer **will be** saved at the LORD's return from the actual presence of sin. See Romans 5:10, Romans 8:18-24, 1 Corinthians 3:15, and 1 Peter 1:3-5.

Those three theological doctrines of salvation are named justification, sanctification, and glorification.

When we talk about salvation, we need to keep all three tenses and all three doctrines in view.

What is justification? Justification means that you have been declared righteous before God because of what Jesus has done. This occurs when you receive the LORD. Justification is by grace. It is a free gift. It is wholly without works. This aspect of salvation cannot be reversed or lost. You cannot lose your justification.

The second idea, the doctrine of sanctification, pertains to your growth. Now **read this carefully**. You **can lose** this aspect of your salvation by refusing to grow in righteousness. You need to note the difference between positional sanctification and practical sanctification. There is a difference between our position and our practice.

Our **position** is our foundation, what we build on. Our positional sanctification is built upon the foundation of justification. Once we are justified, then, based on this, God considers us totally sanctified. That means we have been totally set apart for His use (See 1 Corinthians 1:2 and 6:11); and, therefore, glorification (our future reward) is guaranteed. That is our position from God's perspective. This is how God sees us.

But there is another aspect called our **practice**. Our practice is what happens on a day-to-day basis here in this world. In position we are justified by God, but then we are told to build upon the foundation (see 1 Corinthians 3:12-15) that we have received on a practical day-to-day basis.

To practice our faith means that we have to study the Word of God and then put it to work. In other words, we have to live the Word of God daily by obeying what we have learned. We can choose to obey God or disobey God. When we choose to submit to God and obey Him, we will find our behavior and character slowly molded into the image of Christ. If we obey consistently, our growth will come faster. If we obey erratically and partially, our growth will come at a slower pace.

Now we come to the concept of glorification. Glorification has to do with the rewards we will receive in eternity. Glorification is tied into the amount of obedience—and trust, faith, and growth—that we have experienced during our walk with the LORD. We will each be rewarded differently according to how much we have obeyed what we were asked to do.

So, in position, you cannot lose your sanctification, but in practical day-to-day experience, you can lose this aspect of salvation if you choose to live in a carnal lifestyle, to walk away from the LORD, or not to grow and exhibit faith in Him. You will lose the rewards you might have had, and you will lose out on the sanctification aspect of your salvation. Remember, you cannot lose the justification aspect of your salvation, but you can lose, in a practical sense, the sanctification aspect of salvation if you choose not to grow.

Again, read this carefully! I need to repeat the material because it is so important. We can lose our rewards depending on our growth, depending on our sanctification. However, our eternal state is secure because that is based only on our faith in Jesus. It is based on what Jesus did for you and me; it is based on our justification. Therefore, our glorification is guaranteed, but the amount of glorification or rewards we receive will vary if we do not live the faithful, righteous life of a believer.

We hope you do not think we are saying that you can be justified or saved and then live any way you want or that you can be saved and then live like the devil. You will suffer if you do. There will be punishment and discipline meted out to you from the LORD. We are expected by God to perform good works. We are saved for good works in order to glorify God. We are justified and then we are to live, work, and struggle to be righteous in our daily life. And if we do, we will receive tremendous rewards when we are glorified.

When a person believes that that it is possible to lose one's salvation, that person is confusing the two concepts of justification and sanctification. To put it in simple terms, you cannot lose your justification, but you can lose your sanctification. When you read verses that seem to indicate that your eternal future is not secure, take another look at them. You will find that they are talking about sanctification (your walk) rather than justification (God's gift). You are secure eternally in Messiah, and no one (not even yourself) can snatch you out of His strong, loving hand.

Romans 8:28-30

> And we know that God causes all things to work together for good to those who love God, to those who are called according to His purpose. For those whom He foreknew, He also predestined to become conformed to the image of His Son, so that He would be the firstborn among many brethren; and these whom He predestined, He also called; and these whom He called, He also justified; and these whom He justified, He also glorified.

John 10:27-30

> "My sheep hear My voice, and I know them, and they follow Me; and I give eternal life to them, and they will never perish; and no one will snatch them out of My hand. "My Father, who has given them to Me, is greater than all; and no one is able to snatch them out of the Father's hand. "I and the Father are one."

10. COURTYARD AND THE OIL

COURTYARD DESCRIPTION

God describes the courtyard to Moses in Exodus 27:9-12:

> You shall make the court of the tabernacle. On the south side *there shall be* hangings for the court of fine twisted linen one hundred cubits long for one side; and its pillars *shall be* twenty, with their twenty sockets of bronze; the hooks of the pillars and their bands *shall be* of silver. Likewise for the north side in length *there shall be* hangings one hundred *cubits* long, and its twenty pillars with their twenty sockets of bronze; the hooks of the pillars and their bands *shall be* of silver. *For* the width of the court on the west side *shall be* hangings of fifty cubits *with* their ten pillars and their ten sockets.

The Tabernacle itself was situated inside a courtyard that was bounded by a linen fence (see Figure 12). This courtyard was one hundred fifty feet long, seventy-five feet wide, and approximately seven and one half feet high, as we'll learn in verse 18.

This fence was made of fine twisted linen. Again we find the word *shesh* here--the highest quality linen that Egypt could produce, higher than we produce today. These were just simple, plain, white curtains. The linen was woven creating curtains one hundred fifty feet long and seven and one half feet high. There were posts spaced at regular intervals along the perimeter of the courtyard. These posts were made of acacia wood and fitted into bronze bases or sockets. There were silver hooks on the posts and silver rods at the top of

Figure 12. The Temple and Courtyard

each post rigidly joining the rods together. The linen curtains were suspended on these rods that went between the posts from post to post. Notice again that as we retreat away from the Holy of Holies, the material used in the construction of the Tabernacle becomes less precious in value. Here we have wooden pillars, not overlaid with silver or gold. We have bronze bases on the outside of the compound and not silver bases like we found inside the Tabernacle.

Continuing to read Exodus 27:13-16 we learn:

> And the width of the court on the east side *shall be* fifty cubits. The hangings for the *one* side *of the gate shall be* fifteen cubits *with* their three pillars and their three sockets. And for the other side *shall be* hangings of fifteen cubits *with* their three pillars and their three sockets. For the gate of the court *there shall be* a screen of twenty cubits, of blue and purple and scarlet *material* and fine twisted linen, the work of a weaver, *with* their four pillars and their four sockets.

The east end formed the entrance to the Tabernacle compound. Curtains twenty-two-and-one-half feet wide extended from the corners toward the middle of the fence. This left an open space of thirty feet as an entrance to the Tabernacle courtyard.

In order to cover this opening, a special curtain 30 feet long was now woven. This curtain was not plain white like the rest of the courtyard linen, but woven of blue, purple, and scarlet linen, creating a very different and colorful gate to the Tabernacle compound. This screen of blue, purple, and scarlet linen was of the highest quality cloth available. These colors would stand out and clearly identify the entrance of the compound.

Note verse 16 where the four pillars are mentioned. I once saw a poster of the Tabernacle, and the artist had labeled these four pillars Matthew, Mark, Luke, and John. However, this is just the imagination of the artist because there is no biblical warrant for making that connection. To do this is also very weak when you think about the coming Temple because that Temple will have no pillars at the entrance, so immediately this symbolism of Matthew, Mark, Luke, and John disappears This is an area of doubtful symbolism, and we do not recommend that you go down that route when you look at the Tabernacle or the Temples.

A further description of the courtyard is made in Exodus 27:17-19:

> All the pillars around the court shall be furnished with silver bands *with* their hooks of silver and their sockets of bronze. The length of the court *shall be* one hundred cubits, and the width fifty throughout, and the height five cubits of fine twisted linen, and their sockets of bronze. All the utensils of the Tabernacle *used* in all its service, and all its pegs, and all the pegs of the court, *shall be* of bronze.

Apparently, various other miscellaneous items were to be made, all pertaining to the functioning of the Tabernacle on a day-to-day basis. Its setting up, its tearing down, its structure, and a lot of other details are left out for us, but these behind-the-scenes little pieces of the Tabernacle were all made of bronze.

The only items specifically mentioned were the bronze tent pegs. This indicates to us that the pillars were supported on either side by guy wires; in other words, ropes were attached to the top of the posts and secured to the pegs in the ground. This stabilized the posts side to side while the silver rods between the posts stabilized them all along the length of the compound.

Again, this is another place where we come to some doubtful symbolism. In the drawing I mentioned earlier, the pegs and the guy wires were labeled as the sustaining power of Christ. This is obviously a reference to the fact that the pegs and the guy wires helped sustain and stabilize the posts. But again, when you move from the Tabernacle to the Temple, you find that there were no pegs or guy wires in the Temple. Does this mean that when we move to the Temple, the sustaining power of Christ is gone? Any symbolism used really ought to be consistent from Tabernacle to Temple. Please do not try to find some kind of meaning in every single detail of the Tabernacle. God chose not to tell us all the fine points of the Tabernacle. We do not need to labor to attach spiritual significance to everything.

Historical Significance

In the courtyard, the fence taught the principle of separation and limited access to God. Only Jewish people were allowed access through the fence, through that brightly covered gateway. No gentiles (non-Jews) were allowed to enter.

Another significant point is that those worshipping in the Tabernacle faced west. The Tabernacle is very specifically aligned in an east/west direction. Those who entered the Tabernacle entered from the eastern side facing west. As a result, they had their backs to the rising sun. This is significant because through this orientation, God shows his displeasure at those who worship the sun. Normal sun worshippers prostrated themselves face down on the ground facing east, facing the rising sun. The orientation of the Tabernacle, and later of the Temples, revealed there was only one true God to worship, not the sun or the moon or the stars.

Worshipping other gods was a problem for Israel. The problem of sun worship is highlighted in the book of Ezekiel when Ezekiel experiences a vision of the wickedness in the Temple. Ezekiel is in Babylon, and in his vision he is transported in spirit to Jerusalem, which is still standing, not yet destroyed by the Babylonians, as described in Ezekiel 8:16-18:

> Then He brought me into the inner court of the Lord's house. **[Ezekiel has been transported to the inside court of Solomon's temple.]** And behold, at the entrance to the temple of the Lord, between the porch and the altar, *were* about twenty-five men with their backs to the temple of the Lord, and their faces toward the east; and they were prostrating themselves eastward toward the sun. He said to me, "Do you see this, son of man? Is it too light a thing for the house of Judah to commit the abominations which they have committed here, that they have filled the land with violence and provoked Me repeatedly? For behold, they are putting the twig to their nose [a sun worshiper's ritual offensive to God]. Therefore, I indeed shall deal in wrath. My eye will have no pity nor will I spare; and though they cry in my ears with a loud voice, yet I will not listen to them."

There is only one God, and there is only one way of salvation. Worshipping another so-called god is not a trivial matter. A lot of people say, "Well, you have your religious belief, and I have mine, and that is fine for you, and it is fine for me. We will just be one big happy family." That type of thinking is simply not true. It matters a great deal. It is the difference between truth and falsehood. Who you worship is very important. There is only one God and one way to salvation. If you worship anything other than the true God, you are worshipping falsehood, a lie. The people Ezekiel saw were worshipping a lie.

The last historical point is that the multi-colored linen gate to the courtyard spoke of authorized entrance into the courtyard. Remember, the multi-colored linen is identified with the King. Those who wore the King's colors were identified as the King's representatives, and they were important community figures.

For example, let's look at Tamar, one of the daughters of David. She was an Israeli princess, a royal girl, who was raped by her brother. Second Samuel 13:18-19 reads:

> Now she had on a long-sleeved garment; for in this manner the virgin daughters of the kings dressed themselves in robes. Then his attendant took her out and locked the door behind her. Tamar put ashes on her head and tore her long-sleeved garment which *was* on her; and she put her hand to her head and went away, crying aloud as she went.

The point is this special garment identified Tamar as a princess; she was not an ordinary person. It was the same with Joseph in Genesis 37:2-4:

> These are *the records of* the generation of Jacob. Joseph, when seventeen years of age, was pasturing the flock with his brothers while he was *still* a youth, along with the sons of Bilhah and the sons of Zilpah, his father's wives. And Joseph brought back a report about them to their father. Now Israel loved Joseph more than all his sons, because he was the son of his old age; and he made him a varicolored

tunic. His brothers saw that their father loved him more than all his brothers; and *so* they hated him and could not speak to him on friendly terms.

This richly ornamented coat, this colored tunic that Jacob gave to Joseph, identified him as the heir of the family and the authority. He stood out in the community and the family because of these clothes. And so his older brothers hated him. He had cut into the inheritance line ahead of them.

The same picture is being portrayed here by the entrance curtain. The richly ornamented entrance curtain identified the only authorized entrance into the courtyard of the King. Just as David's daughter, Tamar, was identified with the king through her garb, and just as Joseph was identified as the heir apparent of his family through the brightly colored robe, so the entrance curtain with its bright colors identified the entrance into the courtyard of the King.

Messianic Significance

The symbolism of the courtyard has significance for us today. The separation of Jew from gentile was broken down by Messiah's death. Remember that gentiles were excluded from the courtyard of the Tabernacle. They were only allowed to come up *to* the courtyard. This was true too in the Temple. There was a court of the gentiles in the compound, but there was a dividing wall that the gentiles could not pass beyond. All this separation of gentiles from Jews was broken down through the death of Messiah. Paul wrote to the gentiles in Ephesians 2:12:

> *Remember* that you were at that time separate from Christ, excluded from the commonwealth of Israel, and strangers to the covenants of promise, having no hope and without God in the world.

That is not exactly the way the other religions of this world would like to picture themselves, and it is not a very complimentary description of mankind, and especially a religious person out in the world. Some of the words Paul used are *separated, excluded, strangers* to the covenant, and *no hope* without God. That is where all gentiles are when they are outside of Messiah.

But, praise the LORD, in Ephesians 2:13-14, Paul says:

> But now in Christ Jesus you who formerly were far off have been brought near by the blood of Christ. For He Himself is our peace, who made both *groups into* one and broke down the barrier of the dividing wall.

The dividing wall of hostility, pictured by the fence around the courtyard, has been broken down, breached, by the death of the Messiah.

The orientation of the Tabernacle teaches the truth that there is only one God. Jesus is God, and He as God is the only one we should worship. We worship God the Father through God the Son. Believers should not be involved in false worship of any kind.

1 John 5:20 tells us:

> And we know that the Son of God has come, and has given us understanding so that we may know Him who is true; and we are in Him who is true, in His Son Jesus Christ. This is the true God and eternal life.

John very clearly lays out the truth for us. This is the true God and eternal life, Jesus Christ. Then he closes with this very telling comment in 1 John 5:21:

> Little children, guard yourselves from idols.

Do not get involved in any kind of false worship. Worship only Jesus!

The final point under Messianic significance deals with the fact that Jesus is the door. He is the entrance into forgiveness; He is the entrance into fellowship with God. John 14:6 gives us this truth:

> Jesus said to him, "I am the way, and the truth, and the life; no one comes to the Father but through Me."

Acts 4:12 supports that statement:

> And there is salvation in no one else; for there is no other name under heaven that has been given among men by which we must be saved.

There is no other way! There is only one way! Just as there is only one authorized entrance into the Tabernacle, even so Jesus is the one spiritual door, the only authorized access to God. He is the one way into forgiveness and fellowship with God.

It is absolutely not true that there are many ways to God. There is only one way, and that is personal faith in Israel's Messiah, *Yeshua* (Jesus).

Application

It is important to ask some very practical questions at this point. The first is for Jewish Christians. "How do I relate to my gentile brothers and sisters in the Lord? Do I make my gentile brothers and sisters feel second-class in my Messianic congregations?"

You may be aware that Jewish people who become believers sometimes prefer to maintain their Jewish heritage in their worship. They choose to meet in Messianic Jewish congregations where they observe biblical holidays and worship with Jewish liturgy. Before becoming a full-time Bible teacher at HaDavar Messianic Ministries, I was a Messianic pastor for seven years, and it was a struggle to be sure the gentile brothers and sisters were not made to feel inferior because they were attending a Messianic congregation. We have to be very careful to avoid cultural idolatry.

I used to tell the people in my congregation that Jesus-ness comes before Jewish-ness. *Yeshua-ness* comes before Jewish-ness. We should not worship our cultural identity. We can be proud of our culture and practice the things that our culture does, but we should not make others feel second class. I must ask myself if I exclude my gentile brothers and sisters in my congregation. Has the wall of partition been truly broken down in my life?

Let us turn this around and put the shoe on the other foot. The same goes for gentile believers. If you are a gentile, do you make your Jewish brothers and sisters feel second class in your church? This can easily happen as well.

A second question to ask is, "Am I letting something other than God become more important in my life? Am I, in essence, exchanging God for something else? Am I turning my back on Him unwittingly? Do I turn my back on materialism or New Age thinking or the occult or anything else that distracts me from God?"

We need to turn our faces toward Jesus. Remember what John said about Him being the true God who gives eternal life. Guard yourself from idols and distraction from God. You must keep your face firmly turned toward Him and your eyes firmly focused on Him.

OIL DESCRIPTION

Next comes a discussion of the use of oil in the Tabernacle. The Tabernacle compound has been described from inside to out, but now another description takes us back into the Holy Place. Exodus 27:20-21 begins with a description of the oil to be used in the Tabernacle:

> You shall charge the sons of Israel, that they bring you clear oil of beaten olives...

A fine, clear oil is to be brought to the Tabernacle. How is this oil gathered? Olives were harvested and then crushed in an olive press. The very first flow of oil that was obtained in that manner was the finest, clearest, highest quality oil obtainable.

The second part of Exodus 27:20 covers the purpose for the oil:

> ...for the light, to make a lamp burn continually.

The oil was for light to be provided for the Holy Place.

In Exodus 27:21, God gives a charge:

> In the tent of meeting, outside the veil which is before the testimony, Aaron and his sons shall keep it in order from evening to morning before the Lord; *it shall be* a perpetual statute throughout their generations for the sons of Israel.

God specifically instructs that the lamps, fueled by the olive oil, were to be kept burning in the Holy Place so there would always be light and the Holy Place would never be dark.

The light is called *ner tamid* which means a continual light. This is where we get the practice of *ner tamid,* or having a light burning continually in the synagogue.

Another name for the Tabernacle is brought out in verse 21. It was called "the tent of meeting." The Hebrew is *ohel moed.*

Ohel means tent. This emphasizes the temporary structure of the Tabernacle. It was temporary in the sense of being portable and also in the sense that it would not last forever. It would eventually be replaced by a permanent structure, the Temple.

The word *moed* simply means meeting. This emphasized what happened in the Tabernacle. Here God met with Israel through Israel's representative, the High Priest.

Please notice also the term *perpetual statute* in that verse as rendered here in the New American Standard Bible. The same term is rendered as *lasting ordinance* in the New International Version. In the Hebrew the term is *hukaht olam*.

Hukaht is a form of the word *hoke*, and *hoke* has a broad spectrum of meaning. A *hoke* can mean statute, ordinance, law, decree or custom.

The other word is *olam* and simply means a very long time or an age. What God is saying here is that this commandment or practice will last for a period of time or an age. A better translation would be a "long-lasting" or "age-long" ordinance or statute. The age or time period being described is the period of the Mosaic Law or Mosaic Covenant, which lasted from Mount Sinai in approximately 1446 BC until Passover in 30 AD when the Messiah instituted the New Covenant.

Israel, as a nation, has not yet entered into the New Covenant today. However, individual Jews and gentiles have, can, and are entering into the New Covenant at the present time.

How is this possible? Do you remember reading Jeremiah 31:31-34 a while back? We saw that the essence of the New Covenant is a personal relationship. It is a personal and internal covenant for individuals. Any individual Jew or gentile today can enter into the New Covenant.

However, at the end of the age, *every* living Jewish man, woman, and child will personally enter into the New Covenant. When every Jewish person does that, we will have the national regeneration of Israel. In other words, *the nation of Israel* will enter into the New Covenant.

At this point in our study, we need to ask a very important question that many people are asking today. "Are we obligated to keep the Mosaic Law today?"

That question is clearly answered for us in Galatians 3:19, an important verse that lays out the purpose of the law. In this verse, Paul starts with the same questions we just asked.

Why the Law then?

If we are now living under the New Covenant, and we do not have to keep the Law anymore, was it just something that was extraneous, something that God just put in there that was really never that important to begin with?

Paul gives the answer in the next part of Galatians 3:19:

It was added because of transgressions...

That is a very important phrase. It was added. Added to what? It was added to the Abrahamic Covenant. The Abrahamic Covenant preceded the Law of Moses by quite a number of years. The Abrahamic Covenant is an unconditional and eternal covenant. So the Law then was *added to* the Abrahamic Covenant. Paul goes on to say it was because of transgressions. The Mosaic Law was added in order to deal with the issue of sin, in order to provide behavior boundaries for Israel. These practical boundaries were given to show how to live an upright and righteous life on a daily basis. The Mosaic Law came into existence at Mount Sinai about 1446 BC. Next we read in Galatians 3:19:

> ...having been ordained through angels by the agency of a mediator, until...

When we read the word *until,* we know that the Mosaic Law also has an ending. Until when?

> ...until the seed would come to whom the promise had been made.

The seed who was to come is a reference to Jesus the Messiah. The timeframe for the word *until* is the year 30 AD when Jesus the Messiah instituted the New Covenant during Passover. From 1446 BC to 30 AD was the approximate time duration of the Mosaic Law.

We are no longer under the Mosaic Law today. The Mosaic Law prevailed in a certain era of time. That era of time has passed, and the New Covenant is in force to the believer right now.

A lot of people divide the Old Testament and the New Testament up in a rather inappropriate way. They say the Old Testament was a time of Law and the New Testament is the time of grace. That is not really quite an accurate division because there was plenty of grace in the Old Testament. The Old Testament was just a time of unusual demonstration of the Law.

Under the New Testament, we are under grace, so there is an unusual demonstration of grace going on right now. However, we are not totally out from under the Law. Actually, the Law that we are under now is called the Law of the Messiah (Christ). There are obligations to follow in the New Covenant; there are commandments we are to follow. Look at what Paul has to say in 1 Corinthians 9:21:

To those who are without law, as without law, though not being without the law of God but *under the law of Christ*, so that I might win those who are without law.

The point to be noted is that Paul states that he is under the Law of Christ. Let us also look at Galatians 6:2. Here Paul says:

Bear one another's burdens, and thereby fulfill the law of Christ.

The Law of Christ is the Law that we are operating under today. It is fulfilled when we love our brother.

Finally, let us turn to Romans 8:2:

For **the law of the Spirit of life in Christ Jesus** has set you free from the law of sin and of death [emphasis mine].

Here the Law that we live under now is called the Law of the Spirit of life in Messiah Yeshua, in Jesus the Messiah.

We do live under law today, and this may come as a surprise to a number of people. The laws we live under today consist of every imperative or command in the New Testament. An imperative is something to be obeyed. A command is not optional; we are to obey these commands.

A computer search was once done to find every Greek imperative in the New Testament. It revealed that there were well over 600 commands that should be followed by the believer today. While we are living during a time of an unprecedented expression of grace from God, that does not mean that there are no laws. We are to obey the commands of the New Testament; and if we do not obey them, we will suffer discipline. One of the types of discipline we suffer is the church discipline procedure found in Matthew 18:15 and following. If we sin, if we go off on our own track and do not obey our Lord, then the church is given the responsibility to discipline the sinning believer. We are not free to do anything we want. We are to live righteously.

Historical Significance

The Olive Oil

Jesus the Messiah is speaking in Isaiah 61:1:

> The Spirit of the Lord GOD is upon me, because the LORD has anointed me to bring good news to the afflicted; He has sent me to bind up the brokenhearted, to proclaim liberty to the captives and freedom to the prisoners.

When a King or High Priest was set aside for a special task, they would first be anointed with oil. We have seen already that the oil symbolizes the Holy Spirit. Jesus is saying in this verse that He has been anointed with the Spirit of God or the Holy Spirit, which will enable Him to do His task.

The lamp stand and the oil were inseparably bound together. One is useless without the other. Just as the burning oil in the lamp stand provided physical light in the Holy Place, so the Holy Spirit provides spiritual light. The Holy Spirit is the spiritual fuel for spiritual light just as the oil is the physical fuel for the lamp stand.

The lamp stand had seven lamps for which the oil had to be continually provided. The number seven throughout scripture emphasizes the concept of completion and totality; for example, the seven days of creation. When the oil filled the seven lamp stands, it represented the totality of the Holy Spirit.

Messianic Significance

The Oil and Thoughts on the Menorah (Lamp Stand)

The oil symbolizes the fullness of the Holy Spirit that Jesus was to have. Again, that is in Isaiah 61:1:

> The Spirit of the Lord GOD is upon me, because the LORD has anointed me.

Jesus was anointed to do the job. He was not anointed with the symbol. He was anointed with the reality that the symbol portrayed. The oil that anointed the King or the High Priest was simply the symbol of the Holy Spirit, but Jesus was anointed with the reality, the Holy Spirit Himself. Take a look at Isaiah 11:2:

> The Spirit of the LORD will rest upon Him, the spirit of wisdom and understanding, the spirit of counsel and strength, the spirit of knowledge and the fear of the LORD.

This is a Messianic verse. The prediction is that the Messianic person is going to experience the full seven-fold fullness of the Holy Spirit. This verse is nicely pictured as a *menorah* with seven branches (see Figure 13). Think of the center branch of the *menorah* as the Spirit of the Lord. From the center branch comes two branches on each side. Label these inner two branches as *wisdom* and *understanding*. Two more branches extend beyond the inner ones. Label them *counsel* and *strength*. Two additional branches protrude past the middle branches. Label them *knowledge* and *fear of the Lord*. Read this verse with the *menorah* in mind. The Messianic person will experience the seven-fold fullness of the Holy Spirit.

This is exactly how John describes *Yeshua* in John 3:34. John is writing about John the Baptist, the forerunner of the Messiah. There is a little jealousy among John's disciples at this point because Jesus

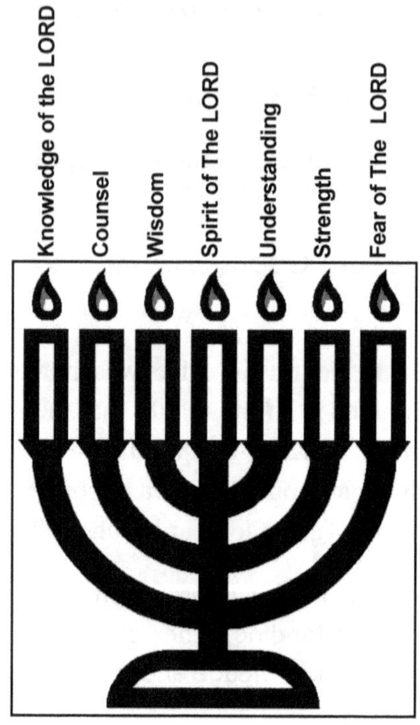

Figure 13. The Menorah and the Holy Spirit

is making and baptizing more disciples than John. John the Baptist rebukes this jealous complaint and explains to his disciples about Jesus, the one who is surpassing him. John 3:34:

> For He whom God has sent speaks the words of God; for He gives the Spirit without measure.

Jesus had the Holy Spirit without measure. We who are simply human have a measure of the Holy Spirit given to us. The Holy Spirit indwells us, and then He empowers us and gives us spiritual gifts. We do not get all the spiritual gifts. Some people have the gift of evangelism, some have the gift of giving, some have the gift of faith, some have the gift of pastor/teacher, some have a combination of two or three gifts, but not all of us receive all of the gifts. This keeps us dependent upon one another. If we all had all the gifts and had the seven-fold fullness of the Holy Spirit, we would not need each other. That is why we receive only a measure of the Holy Spirit. But Jesus, in contrast, because He was the God/man, because He was the Messianic person, because He is the second person of the triune God, experiences the seven-fold fullness of the Spirit as Isaiah 60:1, Isaiah 11:2, and John 3:34 indicate. The oil in these passages is a very appropriate symbol pointing to Jesus the Messiah.

Application

Remember, when you were born again, you received the Holy Spirit as a mark and a seal of your position before God, as Ephesians 1:13-14 states. You were indwelt by the Holy Spirit. You became a dwelling place for God. You became a temple. That is your position in the Messiah.

Now ask yourself some practical questions. "Am I walking in the power of the Spirit who indwells me? If I am walking in the power of the Spirit, am I bearing the fruit of the Spirit as outlined in Galatians 5:16-25? Am I exercising my spiritual gift or gifts in my local congregation?" If you do all that, then you will be able to say that your light is shining before men the way a menorah shines out and the way the lamp stand illuminates the Holy Place. Here is the question again, "Is my light shining out like a lamp stand; is it shining out because I am fueled by the Spirit and bearing the fruit of the Spirit and being controlled by the Spirit?" Being controlled by the Spirit is not automatic. It is a deliberate choice to obey and to live your life in accordance with the righteousness of God, bearing the fruit that God so desires to see in your life.

11. THE PRIEST AND HIS GARMENTS

COMMISSIONING OF AARON AND HIS SONS

Chapter 28 focuses on the priestly garments, the clothes that the priests would wear as they administered in the holy Tabernacle (see Figure 14). The Tabernacle needed a priest or a number of priests to administer the divine services. God takes this position very seriously, which becomes clear as we get a glimpse of the clothes the priests are to wear.

Exodus 28:1 instructs:

> Then bring near to yourself Aaron your brother, and his sons with him, from among the sons of Israel, to minister as priest to Me—Aaron, Nadab and Abihu, Eleazar and Ithamar, Aaron's sons.

The word priest comes from the verb *kahan*. *Kahan* simply means to act as a priest. The noun derived from *kahan* is the word *kohen,* or priest.

By definition a priest is one who officiates and administers divine services. Only God or His official representative can accomplish the atonement by which satisfaction is made for sin. The priest is the one authorized to administer divine reconciliation. In Exodus 28:1, the family of Aaron is chosen for this function.

Figure 14. The High Priest

PRIESTLY GARB

As we move into Exodus 28:2-5, we come to the clothes he is to be wearing. Exodus 28:2-3 describes their purpose:

> You shall make holy garments for Aaron your brother, for glory and for beauty. You shall speak to all the skillful persons whom I have endowed with the spirit of wisdom, that they make Aaron's garments to consecrate him, that he may minister as priest to Me.

The New American Standard Bible (NASB) says "for glory and for beauty," but the New International Version (NIV) says it gives the wearer "dignity and honor." This word *dignity* is the Hebrew word *caved* which means to be heavy. It is a verb. From that we derive the noun *cavod*, which means to be heavy in the sense of noteworthy or impressive. We use the exact same expression when we say, "Wow, that is a heavy concept," or "That is a heavy thought." That is the word translated by the NIV as "dignity" and by the NASB as "glory." The priest was to be viewed as an honored or a weighty person, and the garments of the priest helped to achieve that distinction.

The NASB renders the other word used to describe the purpose as "beauty." The word is translated "honor" in the NIV. The Hebrew verb that is the basis for this thought is the verb *paar*. *Paar* means to beautify, to glorify. From that verb we derive the noun *tifarah* which means beauty or glory. The NASB would be the better translation, "for glory and for *beauty*," rather than "*honor*" as the NIV has rendered it.

A phrase in Exodus 28:3 contains another important word, and that is *consecration*. Look at the phrase again. It says "to consecrate him." The Hebrew word that is the basis for this thought is *qadash*, which means to be sanctified or to be set apart for special use.

As we combine these three thoughts, let's summarize the importance of the garments. The garments were for the purpose of setting the priest apart as a special individual. This distinction was achieved through the beauty and the distinctiveness of the clothing. The High Priest was not to be just a common, ordinary individual. His function as God's appointed and official representative who administered divine services was to be exalted and made distinct.

Going on in Exodus 28:4 we read:

> These are the garments which they shall make: A breast piece and an ephod and a robe and a tunic of checkered work, a turban and a sash, and they shall make holy garments for Aaron your brother and his sons, that he may minister as priest to Me.

Thus there are six total garments.

Exodus 28:5 goes on to say:

> They shall take the gold and the blue and the purple and the scarlet *material* and the fine linen.

The garments are to be made out of the very best that Israel has to offer, cloth woven to beautify the official representative of the King.

Move on to verses 6-8 in Exodus 28:

> They shall also make the ephod of gold, of blue and purple *and* scarlet *material* and fine twisted linen, the work of the skillful workman. It shall have two shoulder pieces joined to its two ends, that it may be joined. The skillfully woven band, which is on it, shall be like its workmanship, of the same material: of gold, and blue and purple and scarlet *material* and fine twisted linen.

Ephod

The ephod was the name of a type of robe or ornamented upper garment. Some commentators think it had sleeves, some think it did not. Some see it as an apron-like garment that was fastened at the waist and went no higher, like a kitchen apron. Whether it went as high as the shoulders or not, all authorities consulted agreed that it extended down to the hips or knees of the priest. Its quality was emphasized by the material, which was the very best, the same cloth that the other items in the tabernacle, such as the inner curtains, were made out of.

The quality of this clothing is also seen in the fact that the craftsmen who wove the clothing were to be skilled. This was not a job given to some apprentice but to highly skilled craftsmen. All this beauty and all this quality identified the wearer as God's representative.

The stones of the ephod are described in Exodus 28:9-12a:

> You shall take two onyx stones and engrave on them the names of the sons of Israel, six of their names on the one stone and the names of the remaining six on the other stone, according to their birth. As a jeweler engraves a signet, you shall engrave the two stones according to the names of the sons of Israel; you shall set them in filigree *settings* of gold. You shall put the two stones on the shoulder pieces of the ephod...

The Hebrew word for onyx is *shoham*. The *shoham* was a semi-precious gem, a variety of agate that has alternating layers of color. The names of the tribes of Israel were engraved on these two stones, six names on one stone and six on the other. These stones were mounted in gold settings and then placed on the shoulder of the High Priest, on the shoulder straps or the shoulder part of the ephod. Why did God command this?

The purpose is found in verses 12-14:

> You shall put the two stones on the shoulder pieces of the ephod, *as* stones of memorial for the sons of Israel. And Aaron shall bear their names before the LORD on his two shoulders for a memorial. You shall make filigree *settings* of gold, and two chains of pure gold; you shall make them of twisted cordage work, and you shall put the corded chains on the filigree *settings*.

These stones were a memorial, a reminder that the priest represented all Israel when he ministered in the Tabernacle. He bore Israel before the LORD on his shoulders when he administered the divine services.

The next verses deal with the breast piece. Beginning in Exodus 28:15-16 we learn:

> You shall make a breast piece of judgment, the work of a skillful workman; like the work of the ephod you shall make it: of gold, and blue and purple and scarlet *material* and fine twisted linen you shall make it. It shall be square and folded double, a span in length and a span in width.

Breastplate

The breast piece is to be made to the same high quality standard as the ephod. Do you see the repetition of this idea over and over and over again? God demands the best.

The breast piece was a span square. A span was approximately nine inches. It was made from fabric nine inches wide and eighteen inches long and then folded in half. This created a breast piece of two layers, two sides, nine inches square, nine inches by nine inches.

The stones of the breast piece are described in verses 17-21:

> You shall mount on it four rows of stones; the first row *shall be* a row of ruby, topaz and emerald; and the second row a turquoise, a sapphire and a diamond; and the third row a jacinth, an agate and an amethyst; and the fourth row a beryl and an onyx and a jasper; they shall be set in gold filigree. The stones shall be according to the names of the sons of Israel: twelve, according to their names; they shall be *like* the engravings of a seal, each according to his name for the twelve tribes.

Twelve precious stones were mounted to this breast piece. There were four rows of stones, three stones to each row. Each stone had the name of one of the tribes of Israel engraved into its surface, so each stone symbolized one particular tribe of Israel.

Let's go on to Exodus 28:22-28:

> You shall make on the breast piece chains of twisted cordage work in pure gold. You shall make on the breast piece two rings of gold, and you shall put the two rings on the two ends of the breast piece. You shall put the two cords of gold on the two rings at the ends of the breast piece. You shall put the *other* two ends of the two cords on the two filigree *settings*, and put them on the shoulder pieces of the ephod, at the front of it. You shall make two rings of gold and shall place them on the two ends of the breast piece, on the edge of it, which is toward the inner side of the ephod. You shall make two rings of gold and put them on the bottom of the two shoulder pieces of the ephod, on the front of it close to the place where it is joined, above the skillfully woven band of the ephod. They shall bind the breast piece by its rings to the rings of the ephod with a blue cord, so that it will be on the skillfully woven

band of the ephod, and that the breast piece will not come loose from the ephod.

Using an arrangement of gold rings attached to the corners of the breast piece plus gold chains and a blue thread, the breast piece was then secured to the chest of the High Priest. It hung from the shoulder pieces and was securely drawn to his chest by the chains and cords going around his waist.

Why in the world would God put all this together and command that it be made for His Tabernacle? Part of the purpose is brought out in verse 29:

> Aaron shall carry the names of the sons of Israel in the breast piece of judgment over his heart when he enters the holy place, for a memorial before the LORD continually.

First, then, this breast piece was to be a reminder of the intimate, covenant relationship God had with His people. Whenever the High Priest went into the Holy Place, he would bear the names of the children of Israel over his heart so Israel was doubly represented before the LORD: by the names engraved on the stones of the shoulder pieces, and now by the names on the stones of the breast piece.

The second purpose for this breast piece was to hold two objects. It was fashioned so that the *Urim* and the *Thummim* would always be accessible to the High Priest when he went into the Holy Place. All he had to do was reach into the breast piece for them. Remember that the breast piece was nine inches square, made of an eighteen-inch strip folded in half. That would form a little pocket, and in this pocket the *Urim* and the *Thummim* would be placed. We read about them in verse 30:

> You shall put in the breast piece of judgment the Urim and the Thummim, and they shall be over Aaron's heart as he goes in before the LORD; and Aaron shall carry the judgment of the sons of Israel over his heart before the LORD continually.

What were the *Urim* and the *Thummim*? In Hebrew, *Urim* and *Thummim* mean lights and perfections.

These objects were the means by which God revealed His will to Israel. As we explain their use, we are going to be using a very important word, *"apparently,"* because very little is known about these objects. Most of our knowledge is sketchy and vague. Here is the best we can say about the *Urim* and *Thummim*. Apparently, it was a method of communicating with God, or a method that God used to reveal His will to mankind. Apparently, the communication with God was limited to yes-and-no questions.

The word "lights" seems to indicate the method by which God would answer. If the answer was *yes*, apparently they would light up. If the answer was *no*, apparently they would remain dark.

Because God was limiting His revelation in this manner, sometimes a number of logical questions would have to be asked before God's will could be obtained. But no matter what the system was, no matter how God communicated to man, the *Urim* and *Thummim* would give the High Priest access to divine revelation. This access might have been basic and limited, but the High Priest still had a direct line to God Himself. By asking a number of yes-and-no questions, he could determine the will of God.

The location of the ephod and the stones over the heart of the High Priest is important. God placed the children of Israel symbolically over the heart of the High Priest because the heart, in Jewish thinking, speaks of the inner man, the essence of man. It also speaks of intimacy of relationship. God is portraying for us how much He cares for and loves the Jewish people. He is committed to the nation of Israel. Not only did the High Priest bear their names on his shoulder, but they also were born before him over his heart. They are part of God's very essence. They have a close and intimate relationship to Him.

Robe

A description of the robe unfolds in Exodus 28:31-34:

> You shall make the robe of the ephod all of blue. There shall be an opening at its top in the middle of it; around its opening there shall be a binding of woven work, as like the opening of a coat of mail, so that it will not be torn. You shall make on its hem pomegranates of blue and purple and scarlet *material,* all around on its hem, and bells of gold between them all around: a golden bell and a pomegranate, a golden bell and a pomegranate, all around on the hem of the robe.

Under the ephod was one of the priest's primary garments. A blue robe extended from the shoulders down to the ankles of the priest. Attached to the hem of this robe at the priest's ankles were cloth pomegranates and tiny golden bells. These items alternated around the hem and served a very significant purpose, which we see in verse 35:

> It shall be on Aaron when he ministers; and its tinkling shall be heard when he enters and leaves the holy place before the LORD, so that he will not die.

The High Priest incurred the penalty of death directly from the hand of God if he entered the Tabernacle without being robed in every one of his vestments. The robe had to be donned so that the tinkle of bells would be heard as he walked. He could not just make it optional. This robe, therefore, has a strong connection with the concept of obedience. It reminded the priest that he had to obey; he had to perform his duties accurately and responsibly.

This robe also gives us the message that the representative of the King could only come into the King's presence if he was appropriately dressed. His obedience to the requirements of God could not be casual; his obedience could not be incomplete. The clothes described here are the daily apparel for the High Priest. He did not wear these clothes when he ministered in the Tabernacle or in the Temple on the Day of Atonement. On the Day of Atonement, he wore simple, white, linen garments when he went into the Holy of Holies. So the ornamental clothing described was the common, everyday garb for the High Priest.

In Exodus 28:36-37 the gold plate is described:

> You shall also make a plate of pure gold and shall engrave on it, like the engravings of a seal, "Holy to the LORD." And you shall fasten it on a blue cord, and it shall be on the turban; it shall be at the front of the turban.

The High Priest's forehead was covered by a golden plate, probably curved, that was an inch or two wide. Carved into the gold were the words, "Holy to the LORD," *Kadosh La Adonai*. This golden plate was secured to his forehead with the blue cord. We might ask why God would specify that this golden plate would have these words on it and be attached in this particular place. The answer is brought out in verse 38:

> It shall be on Aaron's forehead, and Aaron shall take away the iniquity of the holy things which the sons of Israel consecrate, with regard to all their holy gifts; and it shall

always be on his forehead, that they may be accepted before the LORD.

This gold plate emphasized that the High Priest personally bore the guilt of Israel; he is bearing the guilt for sin. Therefore, the gifts of the sinners were acceptable to God.

Tunic, Turban, and Sash

In verse 39-41 we come to the tunic, the turban, and the sash.

> You shall weave the tunic of checkered work of fine linen, and shall make a turban of fine linen, and you shall make a sash, the work of a weaver. For Aaron's sons you shall make tunics; you shall also make sashes for them, and you shall make caps for them, for glory and for beauty. You shall put them on Aaron your brother and on his sons with him; and you shall anoint them and ordain them and consecrate them, that they may serve Me as priests.

The tunic, the turban, and the sash were items of apparel common to all the priests, not just the High Priest. But the purpose was to distinguish these men as special men, to set them apart from Israel as God's official representatives. Not only were the priests to be set apart for honor and distinction through the beauty of their garments, but they were also to be set apart for special service through a formal ceremony. That ceremony is explained in Exodus 29, which teaches that the priests are absolutely and totally to be consecrated to the LORD. The High Priest and the other priests are to be totally set apart for God's service. Nothing is to be held back, absolutely nothing.

Undergarments

As we move on in Exodus 28:42, we come to the undergarments:

> You shall make for them linen breeches to cover *their* bare
> flesh; they shall reach from the loins even to the thighs.

You might wonder why God would go into such detail. The answer is brought out in the first part of verse 43:

> They shall be on Aaron and on his sons when they enter the
> tent of meeting, or when they approach the altar to minister
> in the holy place, so that they do not incur guilt and die.

The main point of these undergarments is modesty. Turn to Exodus 20:26:

> And you shall not go up by steps to my altar, so that your
> nakedness will not be exposed on it.

To act immodestly while administering the sacred rituals of the LORD incurred the death penalty for the priests. God took this very seriously. He issued a direct command. This was in stark contrast to heathen religious practices of the Canaanites who lived in the land the Jews were entering. The Israelites were going into the Promised Land to worship God. The Canaanites were already there with a very sophisticated religion. Their religious practices often included sexual immorality. The Canaanites employed temple prostitutes, both male and female.

God is saying He does not want any heathen practices associated with the priests. God's command comes out in the last part of Exodus 28:43:

> It *shall be* a statute forever to him and for his descendants
> after him.

God very specifically emphasizes the importance He places on obedience to these regulations. The priests and especially the High Priest were not ordinary people. They were set apart to perform special functions for God. This privilege carried with it additional responsibilities that extended to every part of their lives right down to the clothes they wore. Their obedience in every detail of their lives was crucial.

HISTORICAL SIGNIFICANCE

The clothing for the priests signified holiness, sanctification, and being set apart for special use. Everyone knew it the moment they glanced at them. That man is a priest, and that man over there who stands out from the other priests because of his special garb is the High Priest. There was no mistaking who these men were.

The priests were God's chosen and authorized representatives to administer divine services and to administer atonement. It was through them, and especially through the High Priest, that God's wrath against sin was satisfied and reconciliation with God was obtained. This signifies the need for a mediator to come between man and God in order to reconcile them. A mediator had to bear the guilt of Israel. The High Priest and all the other priests were those mediators, and the clothing identified them as such, as God's authorized mediators.

No common person could freely come into the Tabernacle and offer up his own sacrifice and then walk into the Holy of Holies and sprinkle the blood. That person would be vaporized! He would be in total disobedience to God. God ordained the priest to do this for him. And most importantly, on Yom Kippur, the nation needed the mediation of the High Priest more than ever. The High Priest was the only one who could enter the Holy of Holies and administer God's reconciliation.

MESSIANIC SIGNIFICANCE

The most important point to note is that *Yeshua*, Jesus, is our High Priest and our mediator. He is the one who was set apart by God to administer God's salvation. *Yeshua* is the one chosen by God to bear the sins of the world. Let's read Hebrews 9:11-12:

> But when Christ appeared as a high priest of the good things to come, *He entered* through the greater and more perfect tabernacle, not made with hands, that is to say, not of this creation; and not through the blood of goats and calves, but through His own blood, He entered the holy place once for all, having obtained eternal redemption.

Yeshua is our High Priest. Other verses to read along those lines are Hebrews 2:17, 8:1-2, and 6:19-20.

By the way, Hebrews is a very critical book to know. You cannot truly understand the book of Hebrews unless you understand the Hebrew Scriptures, the Old Testament. In Hebrews 8:6 the writer says:

> But now He **[Yeshua/Jesus]** has obtained a more excellent ministry, by as much as He is also the mediator of a better covenant, which has been enacted on better promises.

Yeshua is the mediator of the New Covenant, the one who stands between God and man administering the New Covenant. Hebrews 9:15 tells us:

> For this reason, He **[speaking of Jesus]** is the mediator of a new covenant, so that, since a death has taken place for the redemption of the transgressions that were committed unto the first covenant, those who have been called may receive the promise of the eternal inheritance.

Along those lines, let's read 1 Timothy 2:5:

> For there is one God, *and* one mediator also between God and men, *the* man Christ Jesus...

Jesus is our High Priest, and He is our mediator. He is also our sin bearer. 1 Peter 2:24 tells us:

> He Himself bore our sins in His body on the cross, so that we might die to sin and live to righteousness; for by His wounds you were healed.

Remember that the High Priest bore the sins of Israel on his shoulders and on his chest. Bearing those sins was the concept that the gold plate on his forehead communicated as well. In the same way, Jesus, in a true sense, bore our sins. Other verses to look at are Isaiah 53:4-6, 11.

Hebrews 9:28 adds:

> So Christ also, having been offered once to bear the sins of many, will appear a second time for salvation without *reference to* sin, to those who eagerly await him.

Yeshua bore the sins of many.

We need to understand that when we receive Jesus as our Messiah and Savior, He sets us apart for special use. We become His priests. In 1 Peter 2:4-5 we read:

> And coming to Him as a living stone which has been rejected by men, but is choice and precious in the sight of God, you also as living stones, are being built up as a spiritual house for a holy priesthood, to offer up spiritual sacrifices acceptable to God through Jesus Christ.

First Peter 2:4-5 is written to Jewish Christians. This letter is part of what we would call the Messianic Jewish Epistles, letters written specifically to Jewish believers. In this context of the letter, this verse very clearly points out that Jewish believers will be priests of the Messiah, and part of a holy priesthood. But does that exclude the Gentile believers?

We need to make a distinction at this point because it is very easy to take verses out of context. We believe in the doctrine of the priesthood of the believer. We believe that both Jewish believers and gentile believers will be priests before God. However, we should not use 1 Peter 2:4-5 to prove or to substantiate gentile believers as priests before God. Use instead Revelation 5:9-10 because in the context, it supports the fact that gentile believers are also to be priests of God. This is an important detail of context. Revelation 5:9 states that gentile believers are also priests:

> And they sang a new song saying, "Worthy are You to take the book and to break its seals; for You were slain, and purchased for God with Your blood *men* from every tribe and tongue and people and nation..."

This is speaking of the whole world, and we are focusing in on the gentile part of the whole world. What did Jesus do for the gentile believers? Revelation 5:10 tells us:

> "...You have made them *to be* a kingdom and priests to our God; and they will reign upon the earth."

APPLICATION

So all believers (Jewish and gentile alike) are priests and administer the divine services of the New Covenant (such as, don't forsake the gathering together of yourselves, be a cheerful giver, go into all the world—and to your next door neighbor—and make disciples, love your neighbor as yourself, have integrity). The minute you become a believer, you also become a priest for God.

Practically speaking, we need to ask ourselves, "Am I being a priest for God, today, right now, as I go about my daily walk?"

12. PREPARATIONS: CONSECRATION CEREMONY

PREPARING THE OFFERINGS

Three Animals for Sacrifice

In Exodus 28:43, Moses received detailed instructions regarding the garments to put on Aaron and on his sons and then to consecrate them for the task they had been given. Now, in Chapter 29, we come to the consecration ceremony itself.

The chapter opens with the preparations for the ceremony. Exodus 29:1:

> Now this is what you shall do to them to consecrate them to minister as priests to Me: take one young bull and two rams without blemish...

The first step was to set aside three animals, a young bull and two rams. The key point in this verse is that these three animals were to be unblemished, that is, without defect. In other words, they were to be whole, sound, and healthy. Why do you suppose God made this a requirement? The answer lies in the fact that a whole and healthy animal is a worthy gift to bring to a king, especially if it happens to be the King of kings. For example, God makes this point very clear through the prophet Malachi in Malachi 1:8-9:

> "But when you present the blind for sacrifice, is it not evil? And when you present the lame and the sick, is it not evil? Why not offer it to your governor? Would he be pleased with

you? Or would he receive you kindly?" says the LORD of hosts. "But now, would you not entreat God's favor, that He may be gracious to us? With such an offering on your part, will He receive any of you kindly?" says the LORD of hosts.

Israel had been offering the blind and the sick animals to the LORD as a sacrifice in the Temple, and Malachi asks, "Would you do that to a human governor?" The answer is, of course, "Absolutely not!" In that case, how dare we do that to the King of kings! Would He be pleased with our offering? So the principle ought to be crystal clear to us. If we love and if we respect someone, we will give them gifts that are appropriate and without defect. When your child has a birthday, you do not give that child a broken toy nor a broken birthday present, do you?

God is a person and He wants to be treated with the same love and respect that you desire. That is the whole point of what we call the golden rule in Matthew 7:12:

> In everything, therefore, treat people the same way you want them to treat you, for this is the Law and the Prophets.

That is the first reason for bringing defect-free animals for the consecration ceremony.

The second reason lies in the fact that these animals portray the sacrifice of *Yeshua*; therefore, they have to portray His perfect, sinless character or nature. He was without character defect and the sacrifices should be without physical defect.

In 1 Peter 1:18-19, Peter compares *Yeshua* to a sacrificial animal, "a lamb without blemish or defect." The attributes of these sacrificial animals had to parallel the characteristics of the ultimate sacrifice, Jesus Himself.

Unleavened Bread, Cakes, and Wafers

The next items to be gathered for the ceremony were three unleavened grain products. We learn about them in Exodus 29:2-3:

> ...and unleavened bread and unleavened cakes mixed with oil, and unleavened wafers spread with oil; you shall make them of fine wheat flour. You shall put them in one basket, and present them in the basket along with the bull and the two rams.

These three unleavened grain products were now baked; the unleavened bread, the unleavened cakes that were saturated with oil, and the unleavened wafers that were anointed or spread with oil were all baked.

Three symbols appear here: bread, leaven, and oil. Let's begin with the breads or the baked goods.

Bread in scripture is symbolic of physical provision.

Leaven (or yeast as we normally call it today) in the Bible is a symbol of sin. For example, Jesus used leaven to represent sin in Matthew 16:11-12. Yeshua warned his disciples:

> "How is it that you do not understand that I did not speak to you concerning bread? But beware of the leaven of the Pharisees and Sadducees." Then they understood that He did not say to beware of the leaven of bread, but of the teaching of the Pharisees and Sadducees.

Jesus had told the disciples "beware of the leaven [teaching] of the Pharisees and Sadducees." His disciples had mistakenly taken an over-literal view of His words. Finally they understand after He explained that He was speaking symbolically. *Yeshua* used leaven as a symbol of sin; He used it in its typical, biblical sense. In this case, it was used as a symbol of the sin of false teaching.

In the Talmud, the rabbis likewise declare, "Leaven represents the evil impulse of the heart" (Berachot 17a). So this is a very Jewish concept. Sin, whether it is the evil impulse of the heart or false teaching, is often symbolized by leaven. There is to be no leaven, no yeast, no sin associated with this ceremony; therefore, there can be no bread made with leaven.

Oil is our final symbol. Oil in scripture is associated with the Holy Spirit. We have seen this in Isaiah 61:1.

If you read Exodus 29:2 again very carefully, you will notice that the oil was associated with the bread products in three different ways.

The first bread product here is called *matzo*. That is a Hebrew word meaning unleavened bread. In the first bread product, no oil was present. The second bread product is called *challah*. The oil saturated the dough; it was mixed throughout. The final bread product is wafers. Here the oil was spread or smeared upon the wafers. The Hebrew word that is translated "spread" in the text is *mashach*. *Mashach* means to smear, to spread a liquid, or to anoint. It is from this word that we get the noun *Mashiach*, the anointed one.

As I was reading Jewish commentaries and digging into this section of scripture, I came across an engaging and fascinating statement in both *Rashi's* commentary and *The Soncino Commentary on Exodus*. These are Jewish works, and they agree that the wafers were anointed with the oil in the shape of the Greek letter *chi*. The Greek letter *chi* is very, very similar to our letter *X*. Remember that because we will be coming back to it later.

These three wheat products—bread, cakes, and wafers—carried the idea of sinlessness. They were unleavened. They were just like the animals. They were without defect. In addition, because of the oil, they communicated the idea of being filled with, saturated by, or anointed with the Holy Spirit. In Hebrew, the Holy Spirit is called the *Ruach HaQodesh*.

In Exodus 29:3, everything is to be brought to the entrance of the tabernacle:

> You shall put them in one basket, and present them in the basket along with the bull and the two rams.

All three types of bread were to be put in the basket and be presented with the animal sacrifices.

PREPARATION OF THE PRIESTS

Washing with Water

The offerings are now prepared and are ready to go. In verses 4 through 9, the priests are likewise prepared. Exodus 29:4 states:

> Then you shall bring Aaron and his sons to the doorway of the tent of meeting and wash them with water.

The first step of the consecration ceremony, washing with water, symbolized the removal of uncleanness resulting from sin. This is a very Jewish and biblical symbol. Quoting from the *Pentateuch and Haftorahs* edited by Dr. J. H. Hertz regarding this symbol, Hertz writes on page 344:

> The moral symbolism of the act of washing as the first stage in the ceremony of induction is obvious. Clean hands and a pure heart, according to the Psalmist, Psalm 34:4, are an essential qualification in those who would draw near to God.

That is a nice statement by Dr. Hertz. Cleanliness is an essential qualification in those who would draw near to God.

Dressing in Priestly Garments

Let's move along to Exodus 29:5-6:

> You shall take the garments, and put on Aaron the tunic and the robe of the ephod and the ephod and the breastpiece, and gird him with the skillfully woven band of the ephod; and you shall set the turban on his head and put the holy crown on the turban.

Next, Aaron is dressed in his High Priest garments, the garments we looked at in detail in Chapter 28.

Anointing Aaron with Oil

In Exodus 29:7 we learn:

> Then you shall take the anointing oil and pour it on his head and anoint him.

Now Aaron is anointed with the oil. That word anointed is that word *mashach*. Aaron is anointed by the oil being poured on his head; he is "messiah-ed" and the *Ruach HaQodesh,* the Holy Spirit, will use him in a special way. For the ordinary priest, the oil was not poured. Rather it was smeared with the finger upon the head. What is the point here? Aaron was anointed with much more oil than the common priest. This recognizes the fact that greater responsibilities fell on the High Priest; and therefore, the High Priest was imparted a greater amount of divine blessing instead of being just smeared, so to speak. The Holy Spirit would be poured on him for his greater enablement.

Let's go back to our earlier reference that both *Rashi* in his commentary and *The Soncino Commentary* felt that the wafer of bread was anointed by oil in the shape of the Greek letter *chi*. Both commentaries make the same identical statement in regard to the High Priest's anointing as well. Not only the wafer of bread but also the High Priest's anointing was done with oil in the shape of the Greek letter *chi*.

Quoting from *The Soncino Commentary* (Exodus, page 528):

> One drop of oil was put on his head and another between his eyebrows, and with these his finger traced the shape of the letter X.

The High Priest's forehead was marked with an "x" or the Greek letter *chi*. I am not particularly mystical in nature, but I cannot help but make a connection with the Greek letter *chi* being the very first letter of the Greek word *Christos*. *Christos* is the Greek translation of the Hebrew word *Mashiach*, Messiah. *Christos* is the gentile terminology for Messiah. It comes into English as our word *Christ*.

This is amazing in light of the fact that Jesus is the bread of life and the wafer was anointed with this very same letter. Jesus is also our great High Priest, and High Priests were anointed with this letter. Out of all the letters to choose from, 22 in Hebrew and 24 in Greek, why in the world would the priest and the wafer be anointed with this particular letter? Could God be sending a message here?

Could God be telling us that the one who is the true bread of life and the one who would be the true High Priest would someday also be the one who would administer God's reconciliation to the gentiles? Could God be anticipating all of this through the anointing of the wafer and the anointing of the High Priest with the Greek letter *chi*? That is for you to decide. I am just suggesting the possibility.

Let us move on to Exodus 29:8-9:

> You shall bring his sons and put tunics on them. You shall gird them with sashes, Aaron and his sons, and bind caps on them, and they shall have the priesthood by a perpetual statute. So you shall ordain Aaron and his sons.

Now finally, in this step, the priestly garments are placed upon Aaron's four sons. They are now ready and prepared for the ceremony of consecration.

THE ISSUE OF SIN

We need to emphasize that the ceremony begins at the place where God always begins when he deals with man: the sin issue. Sin separates man from God. For example, Isaiah 59:2 says:

> But your iniquities have made a separation between you and your God. And your sins have hidden *His* face from you so that He does not hear.

Romans 3:9 also says:

> What then? Are we better than they? Not at all; for we have already charged that both Jews and Greeks are all under sin.

That is also the Apostle Paul's assessment of the human condition. Jews and gentiles alike are all under sin. Paul goes on to back up that statement by quoting numerous verses out of the *Tanach*, the Hebrew Bible. In Romans 3:10-18 he goes on to say:

> There is none righteous, not even one; there is none who understands, there is none who seeks for God; all have turned aside, together they have become useless; there is

none who does good, there is not even one. Their throat is an open grave, with their tongues they keep deceiving, the poison of asps is under their lips; whose mouth is full of cursing and bitterness; their feet are swift to shed blood, destruction and misery are in their paths, and the path of peace they have not known. There is no fear of God before their eyes.

Do you get the point? All mankind is mired in the mud and muck of sin. It is not a pretty or complimentary appraisal of mankind. But the words in Romans 3:10-18 are an accurate assessment of unsaved humanity. We see the accuracy because we see mankind's sin acted out everyday all around us and on our TV screens. We read about it in our newspapers. Mankind is dead to God—dead in trespasses and sin, that is, before the sin issue is resolved. The separation between God and man has to be reconciled before the relationship can go any further.

However, the wonder and the beauty of God is that He yearns for reconciliation. He goes out of His way to make it available. If someone wants it and accepts His provision, it is there. That is the greatness and love of our God. The problem lies in the fact that not everyone wants what God provides. Most people reject God's assessment of mankind; and, therefore, they reject His assessment of themselves as sinners. However, there are some people who do look at the world honestly, with their eyes wide open. They see the truth. They are looking for the truth. If you are looking for the truth, you will find it. God will show the truth to you if you truly want to know it.

An example of this kind of person is a man named Ross Cheit. His story appeared in the November 29, 1993, issue of *US News and World Report*. As a teen-ager, Ross Cheit was sexually molested by a male summer camp counselor. He repressed his horrible and painful memories for 26 years until an innocent remark brought them to the surface. The seven-page article in *US News* described his efforts to bring the people responsible to justice. He even spoke with his rapist over the phone. The article closes with a statement by Mr. Cheit that is so relevant to this section of scripture. Mr. Cheit was, at that time, an ethics professor at Brown University. Because of his experience with evil, he wondered if he could go on; he wondered if he could continue teaching ethics, and why. Quoting from the article:

> "They are such moral relativists," he says of his students. "In the midst of this whole thing, one of my seniors asked, 'Aren't these moral taboos just cultural constructions. Isn't incest bad just because we think it is?' I wanted to shake her and say, 'There is evil in the world; I just got off the phone with it.'"

Ross Cheit has reached the right conclusion. There is evil in the world, and you can talk with it on the phone. You can talk with it face-to-face. You and I know it, you and I experience it. We are part of it, and the Bible teaches it as well. Jeremiah 17:9 says:

> The heart is more deceitful than all else and is desperately sick; who can understand it?

We are capable of perpetrating the most violent sins and then just casually explaining away our evil deed. It only takes the right opportunity.

For example, when I was a soldier in Vietnam, I knew a lot of young men my age: 19, 20, 21. They were just kids back on the block when they were in the states. But some of them, when they were in Vietnam, took advantage of their license to kill. One man I knew loved to fire his weapon—loved to kill people—and he said that he was going to go back to Vietnam as a mercenary when his tour of duty with the US Army was over. One of my friends asked him, "Whose side are you going to be on?" And he said, "Whoever will pay me the most money." Here he was, just a kid on the block in the

States. But he became a killer for hire when he was given permission to do it in Vietnam.

We are capable of perpetrating the most violent sins and then casually explaining away our evil deed. The only thing that has turned us away from the evil in this world and in ourselves is the loving and gracious intervention of God. We have been saved by our loving, heavenly Father. This is why God's consecration ceremony begins by dealing with the issue of sin. No one can be God's priest— no one can administer God's reconciliation to another—unless he or she is first reconciled to God. This is not something dreamed up by some gentile theologian in order to lead gullible Jewish people astray. Quoting Rabbi Hertz from the *Pentateuch and Haftorahs* (page 344):

> The priests must themselves have undergone atonement for their transgressions before they can perform the ceremony that would help others to gain purification from sin.

Biblical faith recognizes the estrangement from God that results from sin as well as the provision of God to end that alienation. For that reason, the key element in the consecration ceremony was a series of sacrifices.

13. CONSECRATION CEREMONY

ANIMAL SACRIFICES

The Bull: The Sin Offering

We begin in Exodus 29:10 with the sacrifice for sin:

> Then you shall bring the bull before the tent of meeting, and Aaron and his sons shall lay their hands on the head of the bull.

The first step was to bring the young bull to the entrance of the Tabernacle. Aaron and his sons then placed their hands upon the head of the animal and leaned upon it. The rabbis teach that "one's whole force," one's whole weight was to rest upon the sacrifice.[6] This leaning on the sacrifice is symbolic of substitution and identification. This is God's method of dealing with sin. God's wrath burns against sin; God's wrath demands the death of a sinner. The soul who sins is the one who will die (Ezekiel 18:20). Yet God, in his gracious, patient love permits a worthy substitute to die in place of the sinner. This animal was going to die that substitutionary death. The bull was not guilty of sin, but since Aaron and his sons had to live in order for the Tabernacle to function, a substitute had to die. By leaning upon the bull with their full weight, Aaron and his sons were saying, "This is my substitute; it is bearing the full weight of my sin." And undoubtedly, Aaron and his sons confessed their sins while they leaned upon the animal. In fact, during the Second

---

[6] A. Edersheim, *The Temple: Its Ministry and Services*, Electronic Ed., 2002, E-4 Group, page 114. Also view entire text online at *http://philologos.org/__ eb-ttms/default.htm.*

Temple period there was a traditional prayer repeated by the sinner as he leaned with his whole weight upon the animal:

> I entreat thee oh, Jehovah. I have sinned; I have done perversely. I have rebelled. I have committed—and he names the sin—but I turn in repentance. Let this be for my atonement.[7]

Exodus 29:11 reads:

> You shall slaughter the bull before the LORD at the doorway of the tent of meeting.

The Jewish method of sacrifice was not painful to the animal. Without question, the animal died. But its death did not come in a cruel manner.

How was the animal sacrificed? First of all, the animal's snout was elevated by stretching the neck and exposing the windpipe and the major arteries in the neck. Then a razor sharp knife was drawn swiftly across the neck severing the windpipe and the arteries. The animal felt little or no sensation from the incision and instantly blacked out because of the immediate loss of blood pressure to the brain. If you have any concerns about brutality to animals, please rest assured that God has not commanded senseless cruelty through the sacrificial system.

We read further in Exodus 29:12:

> You shall take some of the blood of the bull and put it on the horns of the altar with your finger; and you shall pour out all the blood at the base of the altar.

---

[7] A. Edersheim, *The Temple: Its Ministry and Services*, page 82.

After the jugular vein had been severed, the heart continued to beat, and that pumped blood out of the body. The blood was caught in vessels by the officiating priest. The vessel of blood was carried to the altar. Some of the blood was smeared upon the horns, and the remaining blood then poured out at the base of the altar. This application of the blood testified that the required penalty for sin had been paid. A violent death, a spilling of blood had occurred. God's wrath against Aaron and his sons was satisfied. These sinful men had been reconciled to their absolutely holy God by the death of the substitute. Exodus 29:13 continues:

> You shall take all the fat that covers the entrails and the lobe of the liver, and the two kidneys and the fat that is on them, and offer them up in smoke on the altar.

Next the fat of the bull was collected and burned upon the altar. In Ancient Near Eastern thinking, the fat was the choicest part of the animal, the most desirable part. That is not the way we think in 21st-century America, is it? Today everything we eat is fat-free. However, in Ancient Near Eastern thinking, this was the best part of the animal, and so the best part of the animal was offered up to the LORD.

Next we learn from Exodus 29:14:

> But the flesh of the bull and its hide and its refuse, you shall burn with fire outside the camp; it is a sin offering.

The inferior parts of the animal—the flesh, skin, and dung—are burned outside the camp.

What is the significance of the phrase *outside the camp*? Normally, not always, but normally, the expression means to be sinful, unclean, defiled, humiliated, sick, and disgraced. The burning of the inferior parts of the bull outside the camp symbolized that the sins of Aaron and his sons had been removed or had been taken away. Unclean, defiling, disgraceful sin had been removed.

This is extremely important in relation to Jesus. Hebrews 13:11-12 tells us clearly:

> For the bodies of those animals whose blood is brought into the holy place by the high priest *as an offering* for sin, are burned outside the camp. Therefore, Jesus also, that he might sanctify the people through His own blood, suffered outside the gate.

The point of Hebrews 13:12 is that whoever accepts Jesus as their substitute, whoever accepts God's sin offering, whoever leans their whole weight against Jesus receives God's reconciliation. They become holy because God's wrath against their sin is satisfied through the death of an unblemished, innocent, worthy substitute. The substitute bears the whole penalty. The sinner bears nothing, yet the sinner receives all the benefit. The sinner becomes reconciled to God through faith. This is God's marvelous and loving provision for our need. Jesus was willing to become our substitute when he shed His blood for us. Jesus was willing to bear the full weight, the full disgrace, the full uncleanness of our sin. And why did He do it? He did it because He loves us. It is as simple as that.

The Ram: A Burnt Offering

With the sin offering complete, we move to the second offering, the burnt offering. The burnt offering involves a different emphasis. The sin offering embraces the idea of confession of sin, forgiveness of sin, and cleansing from defilement. However, the emphasis of the burnt offering is an expression of devotion, an expression of commitment and complete surrender to God. Exodus 29:15-16 tells us:

> You shall also take the one ram, and Aaron and his sons shall lay their hands on the head of the ram; and you shall slaughter the ram and shall take his blood and sprinkle it around on the altar.

The procedure begins in a manner similar to the sin offering. Again, there is the laying on of hands as well as the leaning of the person's entire weight on the head of the animal as a symbol of substitution and identification. This was followed by the slaughter and the application of blood to the altar.

However, the application of blood differed from the sin offering. Instead of being smeared on the horns of the altar, it was thrown against opposing corners so that it fell on all four sides. The next step is described in Exodus 29:17-18:

> Then you shall cut the ram into its pieces, and wash its entrails and its legs, and put *them* with its pieces and its head. You shall offer up in smoke the whole ram on the altar; it is a burnt offering to the LORD: it is a soothing aroma, an offering by fire to the LORD.

After dismemberment, the ram's inward parts were washed, signifying cleansing. Then the entire ram was burned on the altar, given up to God as an expression of devotion, commitment, and complete surrender.

Finally, the burnt offering is described as a pleasing aroma in the New International Version. The New American Standard Bible renders it a soothing aroma. What is the point here? The point is that this commitment of a person's whole life to God—in this case the priest's life—this commitment of dedication is very soothing, very satisfying to the LORD. God has given us a method by which we can understand this satisfaction that He feels deep within His being when someone loves Him fervently. We can understand His satisfaction because we understand the pleasure of a pleasing aroma.

Imagine yourself out in your backyard on a warm summer day. Suddenly the aroma of your neighbor's barbeque drifts over the fence and caresses your nostrils. Mmmm, that smells good. That is your response to the marvelous smell of your neighbor's steak cooking over the coals. It is Ancient Near Eastern aroma therapy. To some small degree, the pleasure that you feel in your heart at that very moment is like the pleasure that God feels in His heart when someone gives their life over totally to Him.

The first ram functioned as a burnt offering to the Lord; it spoke of devotion. The second ram was the actual ram of consecration.

In Exodus 29:19-20 we learn:

> Then you shall take the other ram, and Aaron and his sons shall lay their hand on the head of the ram. You shall slaughter the ram, and take some of its blood and put *it* on the lobe of Aaron's right ear and on the lobes of his sons' right ears and on the thumbs of their right hands and on the big toes of their right feet, and sprinkle the *rest of the* blood around on the altar.

The procedure for this offering begins in a similar manner. Once again, Aaron and his sons lean on the ram, and the ram is sacrificed. This time the application of blood is very different. The blood is first smeared on each priest's right ear, right thumb, and right toe. Two very important pictures are being portrayed for us here.

First, total consecration is being emphasized from head to foot, from ear to toe, and everything in between. The whole man is set aside for God's service.

Second, quoting Rabbi Hertz from *Pentateuch and Haftorah,* page 346:

> The ear was touched with the blood that it might be consecrated to hear the word of God. The hand, to perform the duties connected with the priesthood, and the foot to walk in the path of righteousness. In a kingdom of priests, the consecration of ear, hand, and foot should be extended to every member of the kingdom.

We are to hear, perform, and walk the way God wants us to walk.

In Exodus 29:21 we read:

> Then you shall take some of the blood that is on the altar and some of the anointing oil, and sprinkle *it* on Aaron and on his garments and on his sons and on his sons' garments with him; so he and his garments shall be consecrated, as well as his sons and his sons' garments with him.

Some blood from the altar was mixed with the anointing oil and sprinkled all over the candidates. This act would symbolize that the priests' service would be empowered by the Holy Spirit. They would only be able to serve effectively if they yielded to the control and power of the Holy Spirit, and so their garments would be splattered with this blood and oil mixture.

WAVE OFFERING

In Exodus 29:22-25 we come to the wave offering, the final offering of the consecration ceremony. This offering gave the priests authority to administer the sacrifices. Exodus 29:22 says:

> You shall also take the fat from the ram and the fat tail, and the fat that covers the entrails and the lobe of the liver, and

> the two kidneys and the fat that is on them and the right thigh (for it is a ram for ordination)...

We begin with the choicest parts of the consecration ram. We continue with verse 23:

> ...and one cake of bread and one cake of bread *mixed with oil* and one wafer from the basket of unleavened bread which is *set* before the LORD;...

Now the unleavened grain products are brought forward. Continuing in verse 24:

> ...and you shall put all these in the hands of Aaron and in the hands of his sons, and shall wave them as a wave offering before the LORD.

All these items, which filled up the hands of Aaron and his sons, are waved before the LORD. That is, the hands were moved horizontally in all directions and then vertically. This was a symbol that the elements of the earth were being offered to the God of heaven and earth.[8] Exodus 29:25 reads:

> You shall take them from their hands, and offer them up in smoke on the altar on the burnt offering for a soothing aroma before the LORD; it is an offering by fire to the LORD.

After everything was waved, it functioned as a burnt offering, a statement of devotion and complete surrender to God.

---

[8] Rashi's view. An authoritative English translation of Judaica Press's *The Complete Tanach with Rashi* is available on CD through Davka Corporation, Chicago, IL.

PROVISION FOR THE PRIESTS

The Heave Offering: Food for the Priests

The first provision for the priests is that of food, as recorded in Exodus 26-28. We start with verse 26:

> Then you shall take the breast of Aaron's ram of ordination, and wave it as a wave offering before the LORD; and it shall be your portion.

The only item not totally consumed by the fire was the breast of the ram. This part of the animal was received back by the priests for their personal use. The priests had given over their entire lives to God for His service. God in turn would provide for their needs, for their sustenance from the very work that they performed. We learn in Exodus 29:27:

> You shall consecrate the breast of the wave offering and the thigh of the heave offering which was waved and which was offered from the ram of ordination, from the one which was for Aaron and from the one which was for his sons.

Here a new sacrifice is introduced called the heave offering. The wave offering and the heave offering varied in two ways.

First, they were presented to the LORD in different ways, and second, the part of the animal set aside for the priest was different. The wave offering was moved in a horizontal plane back and forth, while the heave offering was moved vertically up and down.

The wave offering consisted of the choicest parts of the ram along with the right shoulder and breast. However, the heave offering consisted of the right thigh of the priest's ram. Exodus 29:28 says:

> It shall be for Aaron and his sons as *their* portion forever
> from the sons of Israel, for it is a heave offering; and it shall
> be a heave offering from the sons of Israel from the
> sacrifices of their peace offerings, *even* their heave offering
> to the LORD.

The purpose for the heave offering, then, was to provide food for the priests. Since the priests were set aside to administer divine services and to teach Israel, they would not have opportunity to earn a living in a conventional manner. They were employed in ministry full time. God provided for their day-to-day physical needs. The peace offerings of the community would supply their food. The LORD provided for the priests on a very practical level.

Succession

The LORD turns our attention to the provision of another very practical and necessary need, one very few people consider. It is the need for succession. In Exodus 29:29-30 we are told:

> The holy garments of Aaron shall be for his sons after him,
> that in them they may be anointed and ordained. For seven
> days the one of his sons who is priest in his stead shall put
> them on when he enters the tent of meeting to minister in
> the holy place.

So what will happen after Aaron dies? The ordination vestments of Aaron and his sons would be passed down to future generations. The man who would succeed Aaron, the man who would follow Aaron as High Priest, would wear these garments. He would also undergo a seven-day consecration period as part of his succession ceremonies.

Remember, the number seven is important in scripture. It carries with it the idea of completeness or wholeness. The week of consecration ceremonies would portray that the new High Priest was completely set aside for God's service.

This issue of succession is one that a lot of people ignore; however, it is an issue that we all have to face. We cannot do what we are doing forever. Each one of us will die. What happens to our family after we are gone? What happens to our business or our ministry? God does not ignore dealing with this need in the life of Israel. Likewise, we should not ignore dealing with the issue in our own lives. We need to prepare and plan for the good of our families, our businesses, our ministries. It is very appropriate to have wills, trust agreements, and successors—all that's needed for the next generation to move on. That is what God is doing here for Aaron and his sons and for Israel.

Assurance of Fellowship with Consecration Meal

In the next verse, God turns our attention to another seemingly mundane but very important part of the consecration ceremonies, the consecration meal. We read about that in Exodus 29:31-34:

> You shall take the ram of ordination and boil its flesh in a holy place. Aaron and his sons shall eat the flesh of the ram and the bread that is in the basket, at the doorway of the tent of meeting. Thus they shall eat those things by which atonement was made at their ordination *and* consecration; but a layman shall not eat *them*, because they are holy. If any of the flesh of ordination or any of the bread remains until morning, then you shall burn the remainder with fire; it shall not be eaten, because it is holy.

Meals in the Ancient Near East were much more important events than they are in our culture. In ancient Israel, hospitality was a highly esteemed virtue. The guest was sacred. It was an honor to provide for a guest. In ancient Israel, a casual meal would have been very out of place and would have made the guest feel very unwelcome.

In that culture, to eat with someone meant friendship, acceptance, and fellowship. If someone asked you to eat with them, he was saying, "I am your friend, I accept you just the way you are, and I want to have fellowship with you; I want to have a genuine relationship with you."

In addition, the host was responsible for the safety and the welfare of his guests. This characteristic of meals is very clearly seen in Genesis 18:1-8 when Abraham lavishly provides for his guests. He pulls out all stops; he treats them like kings. He rushes around providing for their needs, and then he stands and serves them.

All these thoughts are present in Exodus 29:31-34 in regard to the Tabernacle and to the priests. The meal takes place in God's house, the doorway to the Tabernacle, also known as the tent of meeting. The priests representing Israel are the highly esteemed and honored guests. God is committing Himself to provide for Israel's safety and welfare. God is communicating three messages to Israel through this meal: the nation is His friend, the nation is totally accepted by Him, and He desires Israel's fellowship.

In Exodus 29:33, the New American Standard Bible makes the statement, "…but a layman shall not eat them…." The basic meaning is that a non-priest will not be allowed to eat this meal. It is a rather unfortunate translation. The word "layman" does not really make the point that is trying to be communicated.

Other translations render the thought differently. The New International Version says "but no one else may eat them," and the Revised Standard Version says "an outsider shall not eat of them." The American Standard Version and the King James Version do the best job when they translate the phrase "but a stranger shall not eat thereof."

The Hebrew word used for laymen is *zur* which means to be a stranger. The basic thought is that of non-acquaintance or non-relatedness. In other words, you have to possess the proper relationship to God before you could eat this meal. You have to have the proper personal relationship before you could be consecrated, set apart for His service.

Procedure to Follow

With these basic human needs met (provision, succession, and assurance of fellowship), God now concentrates on the procedure He wants followed for the consecration ceremony. Exodus 29:35-37 deals with the duration of the ceremony and the ceremonial purification itself:

> Thus you shall do to Aaron and to his sons, according to all that I have commanded you; you shall ordain them through seven days. Each day you shall offer a bull as a sin offering for atonement, and you shall purify the altar when you make atonement for it, and you shall anoint it to consecrate it. For seven days you shall make atonement for the altar and consecrate it; then the altar shall be most holy, *and* whatever touches the altar shall be holy.

At least three thoughts should catch our attention. The first is obedience in verse 35. Consecration to God means obedience to His commands. Anything else is inconsistent at best and hypocrisy at worst.

The second thought is completeness, again in verse 35. That thought is contained in the fact that the ceremony lasted seven days. Remember, the number seven in scripture carries the idea of completeness. When this ceremony is over, these men will be absolutely and completely set apart, with no holds barred for God's service.

The final thought in verse 36 is purification. Whenever we deal with God, we always have to take the sin issue into account. God is constantly and unavoidably aware of the impurity and defilement of this world. He is very different from this shattered, broken world that we live in. He is absolutely holy, absolutely undefiled. As a result, everything has to undergo some sort of purification. It must be either ceremonially purified as here, or undergo an actual cleansing, an actual purification, a physical cleansing. Once the atonement for the altar is completed, once the sin issue is completely and totally cleared up, then God is satisfied and the altar can be set aside for sacred use.

Did you notice at the end of verse 37 it says *the altar shall be most holy and whatever touches the altar shall be holy*? This is very unusual. Normally, whenever something unclean touches something that is clean, the unclean contaminates the clean. The clean item becomes defiled. But the opposite is happening here. No matter what it is, if something touches the altar, it is now set aside for God's use. It has a special status because the altar has such special status. This is very different from the norm.

Let's move on to the method that God chose to make atonement, to stop His wrath against sin. Exodus 29:38-42 explains the offerings:

> Now this is what you shall offer on the altar: two one year old lambs each day, continuously. The one lamb you shall offer in the morning and the other lamb you shall offer at twilight; and there *shall be* one-tenth *of an ephah* of fine flour mixed with one-fourth of a hin of beaten oil, and one-fourth of a hin of wine for a drink offering with one lamb. The other lamb you shall offer at twilight, and shall offer

> with it the same grain offering and the same drink offering
> as in the morning, for a soothing aroma, an offering by fire
> to the LORD. It shall be a continual burnt offering
> throughout your generations at the doorway of the tent of
> meeting before the LORD, where I will meet with you, to
> speak to you there.

Here, a brief reference is made to the daily burnt offerings of the Tabernacle service. Two lambs were to be sacrificed; one lamb in the morning and one in the evening. The lambs were accompanied each time by a grain offering of flour and oil and a drink offering of wine.

Verse 42 brings the section to a close by stating that these morning and evening sacrifices were burnt offerings. The Hebrew word for this offering is *olah* which means ascending. The sacrifice was regarded as ascending to God in the smoke while it was being consumed by the fire. When the burnt offering was presented to God, every part of it was consumed by the flames. These offerings signified the complete and absolute dedication of the person presenting the burnt offerings unto God.

By the way, we get the word *holocaust* from the word *olah*. The holocaust of World War II is named after this sacrificial offering. The idea is that the whole sacrifice was consumed by fire.

Apparently, these offerings originated with the priestly installation service and then continued on a daily basis. After this consecration ceremony, these offerings become daily sacrifices on behalf of the entire nation. They were offered every day, morning and evening. They emphasized God's desire that Israel be completely dedicated to Him. If Israel would be completely dedicated to the LORD, great blessing would result. They would find themselves under the blessings of the Mosaic covenant. If they did not follow the LORD wholeheartedly, they would find themselves under the curses of the Mosaic covenant.

In closing, we come to the purpose for the consecration ceremony in Exodus 29:43-46:

> I will meet there with the sons of Israel, and it shall be consecrated by my glory. I will consecrate the tent of meeting and the altar; I will also consecrate Aaron and his sons to minister as priests to Me. I will dwell among the sons of Israel and will be their God. They shall know that I am the LORD their God who brought them out of the land of Egypt, that I might dwell among them; I am the LORD their God.

The basic idea here is the promised blessing of personal and intimate relationship with God Almighty; fellowship with God is on the basis of blood shed for sins. When the priests were consecrated, when the priests were serving the LORD, God would dwell with them. God would give them an audience at the Tabernacle like a king who designates a place where he speaks with his people. The result would be that Israel would know that He is the LORD their God. Israel would experience a personal and intimate relationship with the Creator of the Universe. God, condescending to dwell in a tent, speaks of the depth of His concern and of His love for His people.

HISTORICAL SIGNIFICANCE

The consecration ceremony's significance lies in this thought: In order for Israel's absolutely Holy God to dwell in her midst, proper preparations and considerations had to be in place. Sin had to be dealt with on every level. God's disdain for sin had to be satisfied in every degree. The sin barrier between God and man had to be removed. Then and only then could Israel's King dwell in her midst. Everything—the dwelling place, the priest, and the people—had to be prepared and committed to the King's use.

MESSIANIC SIGNIFICANCE

How does the consecration ceremony relate to *Yeshua*, to Jesus? Jesus is the true, unleavened, sinless bread of life. He was saturated or filled with the Holy Spirit.

We read in John 3:34:

> For He whom God has sent speaks the word of God; for He gives the Spirit without measure.

Colossians 1:19 tells us:

> For it was the *Father's* good pleasure for all the fullness to dwell in Him.

Colossians 2:9 also says:

> For in Him all the fullness of Deity dwells in bodily form.

Jesus is our sinless bread of life; He is saturated with the Holy Spirit. He is God in a human body.

John the Baptist speaks in John 1:29:

> The next day he saw Jesus coming to him and said, "Behold, the Lamb of God who takes away the sin of the world."

Jesus is the ultimate sacrifice for sin, the One Whom the rams and the bulls and the lambs all pointed forward to.

Jesus is also the apex, the top, the pinnacle of the priesthood. He was a Priest who was totally consecrated in the service of God.

We learn in John 10:36:

> Do you say of Him, whom the Father sanctified and sent into the world, "You are blaspheming," because I said, "I am the Son of God"?

Jesus, arguing with the religious leaders, states that the Father sanctified and sent Him into the world. The religious leaders did not like that idea, but Hebrews 9:11 tells us:

> But when Christ appeared as a high priest of the good things to come, *He entered* through the greater and more perfect tabernacle, not made with hands, that is to say, not of this creation.

Jesus is our great High Priest. It is through Him that we meet face-to-face with the King of kings and experience a personal relationship with Him.

In Revelation 21:3-4 John says:

> And I heard a loud voice from the throne, saying "Behold, the tabernacle of God is among men, and He will dwell among them, and they shall be His people, and God Himself will be among them, and He will wipe away every tear from their eyes; and there will no longer be *any* death; there will no longer be *any* mourning, or crying, or pain; the first things have passed away."

APPLICATION

Let us close this section by focusing on the Apostle Paul's statement in Romans 12:1. This is one very potent verse, and it has the sacrifices of Exodus 29 in mind. In fact, the statement refers to any and all sacrifices. The verse reads:

> Therefore I urge you, brethren, by the mercies of God, to present your bodies a living and holy sacrifice, acceptable to God, *which is* your spiritual service of worship.

We have just taken a look at God's mercy. We have seen it expressed in the consecration ceremonies. Now we see God in the form of His Son, in the form of our Messiah, willing to let us load all the weight of our sin upon Himself. He was willing to become our worthy, substitutionary sacrifice and reconcile us to Himself. In view of this incredible expression of love, grace, and mercy, what should we do? Let's analyze this powerful scripture.

> Therefore I urge you, brethren, by the mercies of God, to present your bodies a living and holy sacrifice, acceptable to God...

In view of His mercy, in view of the fact that He makes us into His priests, we need to offer ourselves to Him. He gave Himself to us as our sin offering; we give ourselves back to Him as a whole burnt offering, but not a dead offering. We give ourselves back to Him as a living sacrifice.

> Therefore I urge you, brethren, by the mercies of God, to present your bodies a living and holy sacrifice, acceptable to God, *which is* your spiritual service of worship.

The burnt offering speaks of unqualified devotion and commitment to God. God's desire for our lives is that we give our lives totally over to Him as an act of worship. Our lives should be a living flame, burning brightly upon the altar of love and service. He, in turn, will take our lives and use them to glorify Himself. We do not have to fear this demand of His because He will take care of all our needs, just as the priest received their food from the very sacrifices that they administered. God will take us through the joys and sorrows of this life as we administer God's reconciliation to others, in our home, in our neighborhood, in our work place. As we faithfully serve him, He will in turn provide for us and guide us in His paths of righteousness.

In light of all of this, I need to ask myself, "Have I ever taken Romans 12:1 seriously for myself? Have I ever personally given myself over to God as a whole burnt offering, as a living flame, burning with devotion upon His altar, with smoke ascending to God as totally offered to Him? Have I ever thought of my life in those terms?"

If you have not, we would urge you to consider giving yourself completely to God on the basis of Romans 12:1:

> Therefore, I urge **you**, brethren by the mercies of God, to present your bodies a living and holy sacrifice, acceptable to God, *which is* your spiritual service of worship **[emphasis mine]**.

14. ALTAR OF INCENSE

ALTAR DESCRIPTION

As we move into Exodus 30, God returns to a number of the pieces of furniture and some of the other miscellaneous items that will be very important in the functioning of the Tabernacle.

Fine Materials

Exodus 30:1-2 describes the Altar of Incense:

> Moreover, you shall make an altar as a place for burning incense; you shall make it of acacia wood. Its length *shall be* a cubit, and its width a cubit, it shall be square, and its height *shall be* two cubits; its horns *shall be* of one piece with it.

This is not a very big altar; it is only one-and-a-half foot square and three feet high (see Figure 15). It has that normal design feature of horns on the corners of this altar and again, remember, the horns signify the presence and power of God. Exodus 30:3 goes on to say:

> You shall overlay it with pure gold, its top and its sides all around, and its horns; and you shall make a gold molding all around it.

This entire wood structure overlaid with gold demonstrates once again this altar is made of the best that Israel has to offer. The luxurious gold signifies that this piece of furniture is associated with the great King. This altar is worthy of the King, worthy to be in His palace. As with the other pieces of furniture, there was a decorative and practical molding around the top to keep the incense and the ashes from spilling off. Verses 4 and 5 go on:

> You shall make two gold rings for it under its molding; you shall make *them* on its two side walls—on opposite sides— and they shall be holders for poles with which to carry it. You shall make the poles of acacia wood and overlay them with gold.

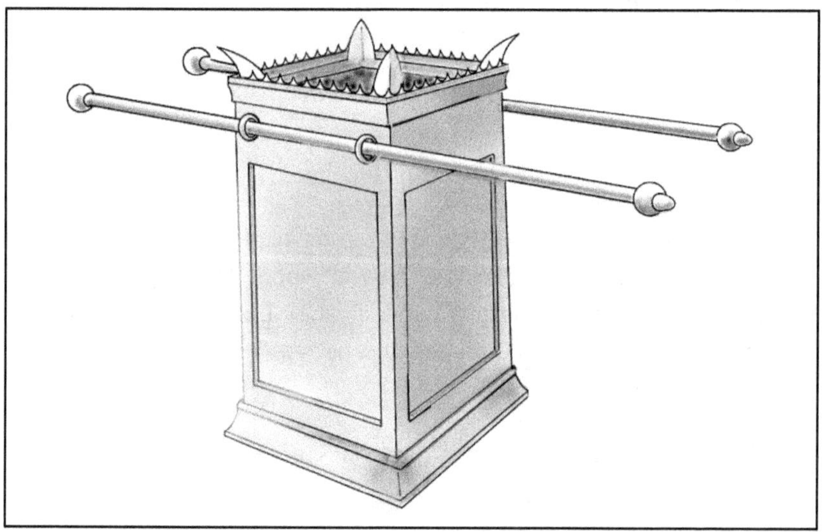

Figure 15. The Altar of Incense

Portability

In keeping with the portable nature of the Tabernacle, the Altar of Incense is designed to be carried with the poles that go through the rings built into the sides of the structure. In verse 6 we come to the placement or the location of the altar:

You shall put this altar in front of the veil that is near the ark of the testimony, in front of the mercy seat that is over *the ark of* the testimony, where I will meet with you.

Offerings

The Altar of Incense stood in the first room, the Holy Place, directly in front of the veil that separated the Holy Place from the Holy of Holies.

Exodus 30:7-10 details the three offerings upon this altar. The first are the daily offerings in verses 7 and 8:

Aaron shall burn fragrant incense on it; he shall burn it every morning when he trims the lamps. When Aaron trims the lamps at twilight, he shall burn incense. *There shall be* perpetual incense before the LORD throughout your generations.

Thus, here are two daily offerings: morning and evening.

How were these offerings made? The priest would take a hot coal from the Bronze Altar in the courtyard, bring it into the Holy Place, and put it on the Altar of Incense. He would then take a handful of incense in a powdered form, and let it cascade out of his hands onto the hot coal. This burning incense would then produce a cloud of fragrant smoke that would fill the Holy Place. Most importantly, it would penetrate beyond the veil into the Holy of Holies, a sweet smelling offering to the LORD.

While the Altar of Incense was placed in the Holy Place (in the outer room), its primary emphasis was that of an offering, an offering in the Holy of Holies in the inner room beyond the veil. There would be a perpetual offering before the LORD throughout all generations. Always there would be incense burning before the LORD. The significance will become clear when we get to the historical aspect of the incense offering.

Issue of Location

Now, let us take a little side trip and discuss the apparent problem associated with the Altar of Incense in Hebrews 9:3-4. Verse 3 reads:

> Behind the second veil there was a tabernacle which is called the Holy of Holies...

That is a reference to the cubical room (a fifteen-foot-square room) in which the Ark of the Covenant was sitting. Verse 4 reads:

> ...having a golden altar of incense and the ark of the covenant covered on all sides with gold, in which was a golden jar holding the manna, and Aaron's rod which budded, and the tables of the covenant.

The problem lies in the fact that Hebrews 9:3-4 seems to place the Altar of Incense within the Holy of Holies rather than in the Holy Place.

The word that causes the problem is the Greek word *thumiaterion,* which is from *thumiaho. Thumiaho* means to burn incense. It comes from that word in combination with *terion. Terion* simply denotes a place. Literally this phrase *thumiaterion* would read "having a place or a vessel for burning incense." This word is translated "Altar of Incense" in most English versions, such as in the New American Standard Bible, the New International Version, the Revised Standard Version, the American Standard Version, and the Amplified Bible.

The one exception is the King James Version (KJV) which translates *thumiaterion* as censer. What in the world is a censer? A censer is a vessel in which incense is burned, especially during religious services. We believe that the KJV has done the best job of translation here, even though the KJV is a minority view. We think that the best translation of Hebrews 9:3-4a reads as follows:

> And after the second veil, the tabernacle, which is called the Holiest of all, which had the golden censer... (KJV)

This is a reference to the High Priest taking a censer of incense into the Holy of Holies once a year as part of the Day of Atonement ritual. Hebrews 9:3-4 is not referring to the Altar of Incense that we are discussing in Exodus 30. A close analysis of the original text solves the problem created by a poor translation.

Let us summarize to try and make this perfectly clear. The reason the word *thumiaterion* means "censer" is three-fold.

First, the word denotes something connected with the burning of incense, so this is a general, indefinite term. Literally, the phrase would mean "having a place or having a vessel for burning incense." That is an adequate description of a censer brought into the Holy of Holies.

Second, in the Septuagint, *thumiaterion* is always used of a censer. The word is never used of the Altar of Incense. When the rabbis translated the Hebrew for censer into Greek, they chose the same word that the author of the book of Hebrews uses, *thumiaterion*.

Finally, the word "having" in the phrase "having a place for burning incense" is an indefinite term that literally means "belonging to." The golden censer was one of the articles belonging to or used for the yearly service in the Holy Place.

The author of Hebrews was not mistaken or confused; he is being quite clear. It is amazing that the King James Version is the only translation to word it this way. The writer of Hebrews is referring to the High Priest entering the Holy of Holies with a censer of incense to burn the offering before the LORD on the Day of Atonement. If you run across this in commentaries or Bible studies, we would refer you to this answer to deal with the problem.

Warning

Let us move on to Exodus 30:9:

> You shall not offer any strange incense on this altar, or burnt offering or meal offering; and you shall not pour out a drink offering on it.

A warning is now inserted regarding possible misuse of the Altar of Incense. Only the correct incense is to be offered upon this altar, nothing else. This warning will go unheeded by two of Aaron's sons in Leviticus 10:1, and it will cause their deaths.

Exodus 30:10 reads:

> Aaron shall make atonement on its horns once a year; he shall make atonement on it with the blood of the sin offering of atonement once a year throughout your generations. It is most holy to the LORD.

This verse covers the Day of Atonement offering, the only exception to verse 9. The other offering to be made on this altar was the application of blood on the yearly Day of Atonement or Yom Kippur.

HISTORICAL SIGNIFICANCE

The Altar of Incense symbolized the prayer of God's people. In Psalm 141:1-2 the psalmist prays to God:

> O LORD, I call upon You; hasten to me! Give ear to my voice when I call to You! May my prayer be counted as

incense before You; the lifting up of my hands as the evening offering.

Do you see the picture here? The vapors of incense rose from the burning coal. They perpetually filled the Holy Place, and they penetrated through the veil into the Holy of Holies. This is a parallel to the way our prayers penetrate from the physical world into the spiritual realm.

Today we cannot penetrate into the non-material, spiritual world in our physical bodies. These physical bodies are not proper to go into the spiritual world. However, our prayers can overcome the physical-spiritual barrier and enter into the spiritual realm where God dwells in unapproachable light.

God wanted His people coming to Him in prayer, constantly, day and night, morning and evening, and He wants us to pray to Him. That is the historical significance of the incense offering.

MESSIANIC SIGNIFICANCE

As we look to Jesus we see He is characterized as a man of prayer. While He was confined to the human body, He spent much time penetrating into the presence of the Father through prayer. As we look at His prayer life, we can discover tremendous lessons for ourselves. For example, in Matthew 14:23 we learn of the importance of private prayer, while in Matthew 19:13 we see prayers are quite appropriate when they are public. In Matthew 26:36-39 we get a glimpse at a type of posture for prayer. In Matthew 26:42-44 we learn lessons about persistence in prayer. In Mark 1:35 we find that we are to pray at any time:

> In the *early morning*, while it was still dark, Jesus got up, left *the house,* and went away to a secluded place, and was praying there.

Luke 6:12 also says:

> It was at this time that He went off to the mountain to pray, and He spent the *whole night* in prayer to God.

We can pray at any time for any length of time, even all night if we need to.

In John 17:1 Jesus is celebrating the Passover, and we see Him pray the High Priestly Prayer.

So the Altar of Incense represents Jesus, a man characterized as a man of prayer. Please read these sections of scripture, and you will learn wonderful lessons about prayer for your life.

APPLICATION

This same symbolism of our prayers being represented by the incense is brought out in the New Covenant, the *Brit Hadashah*. We see in Revelation 5:8:

> When He had taken the book, the four living creatures and the twenty-four elders fell down before the Lamb, each one holding a harp and golden bowls full of incense, which are the prayers of the saints.

We see this same picture in Revelation 8:3-4:

> Another angel came and stood at the altar, holding a golden censer; and much incense was given to him, so that he might add it to the prayers of all the saints on the golden altar which was before the throne. And the smoke of the incense, and the prayers of the saints, went up before God out of the angel's hand.

Here we see in the heavenly realm, an Incense Altar. The prayers of the saints are again pictured as the smoke rising from that Incense Altar. This picture is for you and me today.

Now we need to ask questions such as, "Could my life, should my life, and is my life a life characterized as a life of prayer? What could I do as a believer to follow Yeshua's example and become known as a person of prayer?"

We know we should become people of prayer, but there is a warning that goes along with prayer found in James 4:1-3:

> What is the source of quarrels and conflicts among you? Is not the source your pleasures that wage war in your members? You lust and do not have; so you commit murder. You are envious and cannot obtain; so you fight and quarrel. You do not have because you do not ask. You ask and do not receive, because you ask with wrong motives, so that you may spend *it* on your pleasures.

These people to whom James was writing did pray, but they prayed with wrong motives. They wanted God to simply take care of their selfish needs. Their whole view was of themselves. This is the wrong kind of incense to offer on our personal prayer altar. Selfish prayer with impure motives is not the kind of incense that God wants on our altar. Do not pray if your motive is selfish or if you are praying for personal gratification.

14. ALTAR OF INCENSE

15. ATONEMENT MONEY AND THE LAVER

ATONEMENT MONEY DESCRIPTION

Let us now move on to the atonement money found in Exodus 30:11-16. Verses 11-15 describe the money:

> The LORD also spoke to Moses, saying, "When you take a census of the sons of Israel to number them, then each one of them shall give a ransom for himself to the LORD, when you number them, so that there may be no plague among them when you number them. This is what everyone who is numbered shall give: half a shekel according to the shekel of the sanctuary (the shekel is twenty gerahs), half a shekel as a contribution to the LORD. Everyone who is numbered, from twenty years old and over, shall give the contribution to the LORD. The rich shall not pay more and the poor shall not pay less than the half shekel, when you give the contribution to the LORD to make atonement for yourselves."

The numbering of all of men of Israel, twenty years and older, was normally a mustering of the army before going to war. This is a dangerous procedure because it could easily lead to pride. Pride in the might of men could easily lead to reliance on man's resources. We see the danger surface in King David's case in 2 Samuel 24. In that chapter, David takes a census of Israel exclusively for the purpose of ascertaining Israel's military might. David numbers his army against the will of God, and God's wrath burns against Israel.

In verse 12 of Exodus 30, God anticipates the danger. He states that if this numbering of Israel's army is done for the purpose of collecting the atonement money, then no judgment will come upon the nation. The word translated "ransom" in the New International Version and the New American Standard Bible is the word *cofer*. It comes from the word *capar* which means atonement. Atonement, remember, is satisfaction given for an offense or reconciliation after enmity. A *cofer* would be permitted as a substitute that satisfied the offended party and brought reconciliation. This money, because it was for support of the tabernacle, was associated with God being satisfied or reconciled with Israel.

The amount was a half shekel. A half shekel was a silver coin weighing approximately a fifth of an ounce or so. In today's value, that would be about four or five dollars. The key feature of this tax is that all were to give the same amount. The rich gave no more, the poor gave no less. So this tax was quite small, enabling everyone to pay.

But why in the world would God command such a tax? Exodus 30:16 gives us the answer:

> You shall take the atonement money from the sons of Israel
> and shall give it for the service of the tent of meeting, that it
> may be a memorial for the sons of Israel before the LORD,
> to make atonement for yourselves.

We see two purposes for this tax. The first was for use in the construction of the Tabernacle. We learn this in Exodus 38:25-28. All the silver items that were used in the Tabernacle were cast from these silver coins. They were melted down and made into the silver items in the Tabernacle. This money provided part of the raw material for the construction of the Tabernacle.

The second purpose for this collection was to serve as a memorial or reminder of Israel's atonement. That is the point of Exodus 30:16.

Every time you gave the money, every time you paid the tax, you were reminded about your reconciliation with God.

Historical Significance

First of all, the significance of the atonement money was that God's work was to be supported by God's people. God did not go outside of Israel for what He needed for His program. The gentiles were not informed or obligated to pay anything. God's work was supported by the Jewish people, God's people.

Second, the price of atonement was the same for everyone. The amount of atonement money collected was the same amount, no matter whether rich or poor.

Messianic Significance

The price of atonement in the New Testament is the same for everyone, too. The price of atonement is the substitutionary, sacrificial death of *Yeshua*. In the same way, as with the tax, everyone has the ability to pay. The cost of *Yeshua's* sacrifice is faith and trust. Everybody has the ability to place their trust and their faith in Jesus. It does not matter if we are rich or poor, young or old, Jew or gentile, all of us can place our trust in Jesus and receive atonement.

Romans 3:21-24 tells us:

> But now apart from the law *the* righteousness of God has been manifested, being witnessed by the Law and the Prophets, even *the* righteousness of God through faith in Jesus Christ for all those who believe; for there is no distinction; for all have sinned and fall short of the glory of

God, being justified as a gift by His grace through the redemption which is in Christ Jesus.

We're all saved the same way—by placing our trust in Christ Jesus.

Application

Let's ask ourselves some questions. We see that God's work should be supported by God's people so, "Am I adequately supporting my congregation financially?" I can go beyond that question and ask, "Am I supporting other ministries that spiritually benefit me?"

Your congregation should always come first, but if other ministries also benefit you, and if you are able, you should also support them so they can continue to spiritually benefit you and others as well.

You need to consider your money very seriously. The sharing of money, the sharing of resources in the Tabernacle was important to God's work; and it is important in the church and in your daily life as well. Sharing your resources is a very important part of being a person who walks with God. It is an essential part of being in the Body of Messiah. Money needs to be carefully and responsibly administered. Money is not immoral; money is simply a tool that we use to further God's work in the world.

LAVER DESCRIPTION

The Bible describes a large, bronze basin or laver (see Figure 16), that one would encounter after passing the bronze altar in the courtyard, on the way to the Tent of Meeting. Exodus 30:17-18 states:

The LORD spoke to Moses, saying, "You shall also make a laver of bronze, with its base of bronze, for washing; and you shall put it between the tent of meeting and the altar, and you shall put water in it."

No description of the actual basin is given, so we really do not know what it looked like. Jewish commentators feel that it was a large pot with spouts around the side where the water was discharged. If water was not discharged through spouts, then other commentators feel that it was dipped out and poured on the extremities to be cleansed. Most commentators state that in the culture of the day, one did not dip a dirty item into a bowl of water because then you would spoil the entire bowl. Water was very valuable in those days. One dipped out what was needed and then poured that amount over the item to be cleansed. The laver was made entirely of bronze. Bronze would associate the laver with the concept of judgment.

Where did Israel get the bronze? Mirrors in those days were constructed from sheets of smooth, highly polished bronze. The bronze for the laver was collected from the mirrors donated by the Jewish women. We learn this from Exodus 38:8.

Again, we ask the question, why did God provide this basin, this bronze laver full of water? Exodus 30:19-21 tells us:

Aaron and his sons shall wash their hands and their feet from it; when they enter the tent of meeting, they shall wash with water, so that they may not die; or when they approach the altar to minister, by offering up in smoke a fire *sacrifice* to the LORD. So they shall wash their hands and their feet, so that they may not die; and it shall be a perpetual statute for them, for Aaron and his descendants throughout their generations.

In strong repetitive language, God clearly emphasizes the important functions of the laver. The laver was for cleansing. It was absolutely essential that the priests perform their services for God in a state of ritual cleanliness. It was vital that they washed their hands and feet whenever they entered into the Tabernacle, whenever they approached the altar to make an offering to the LORD. Their hands would be soiled from the sacrificial service, so they had to be cleansed. The priests performed their tasks barefoot, so their feet had to be cleansed before entering the Tabernacle as well. From hand to foot, the whole man needed cleansing. This need for cleansing was so important that any breach of this regulation meant death. The laver was placed in the courtyard somewhere between the Bronze Altar and the Tabernacle itself.

The priests had to undergo two types of cleansing. The first was the consecration cleansing as in Exodus 29. That would be a one-time event when they were set aside as priests.

The second type was the daily cleansing that took place during the normal course of their priestly duties, day after day after day.

Historical Significance

There are many symbols associated with water in the scripture. The two most important in regard to the laver are for cleansing (Ezek. 36:24-25) and the Holy Spirit (Isa. 44:3).

Ezekiel 36:24-25 says:

> For I will take you from among the nations, and gather you from all the lands and bring you into your own land. Then I will sprinkle clean water on you, and you will be clean; I will cleanse you from all your filthiness and from all your idols.

Spiritual cleansing is being portrayed here by the physical cleansing associated with the bronze laver.

The second symbol associated with the water is that of the Holy Spirit. In Isaiah 44:3 the LORD says:

> For I will pour out water on the thirsty *land*, and streams in the dry grounds; I will pour out My Spirit on your offspring and My blessing on your descendants.

Figure 16. The Laver

The pouring out of the Spirit is also associated with water being poured out on a dry and thirsty land.

Messianic Significance

The same imagery is carried over into the New Testament. Turn to John 7:37-39. Here Jesus is at the Feast of Tabernacles.

> Now on the last day, the great *day* of the feast, Jesus stood and cried out, saying, "If anyone is thirsty, let him come to Me and drink. He who believes in Me, as the Scripture says,

'From his innermost being will flow rivers of living water.' "
But this He spoke of the Spirit, whom those who believed in
Him were to receive; for the Spirit was not yet given,
because Jesus was not yet glorified.

We see a very clear association of water with the Holy Spirit. This idea of cleansing is also carried over into the *Brit Hadashah* (New Testament), cleansing through the Word of God. In John 15:3 Jesus says:

You are already clean because of the word which I have
spoken to you.

There the Word of God is a cleansing agent for us, just like the water.

The Apostle Paul picks up this same theme in Ephesians 5:25-26. He is speaking to the husbands and says:

Husbands, love your wives, just as Christ also loved the
church and gave Himself up for her, so that He might
sanctify her, having cleansed her by the washing of water
with the word.

As we read and obey the Word, our dirty lives are transformed, and we wash away sinful practices and thoughts. The Word is a cleansing agent.

Finally, in Titus 3:5-6 which speaks of Jesus, we read:

He saved us, not on the basis of deeds which we have done
in righteousness, but according to His mercy, by the
washing of regeneration and the renewing by the Holy
Spirit, whom He poured out upon us richly through Jesus
Christ our Savior.

Again, we see the picture of spiritual cleansing associated with water. You also see the Spirit associated with water. God has poured out His Spirit on us the way the water is poured out at the Feast of Tabernacles.

Application

In pondering these truths, I have to ask myself, "Have I been cleansed by faith in Jesus?"

Just as the priests had to undergo two cleansings, so the believer has to undergo two cleansings. We learn this in John 13:5-10. This was Jesus' final Passover, and the ceremony called "the first hand washing" was approaching. Jesus rose from His place at the table, but he did not wash his hands. He did something very different. We read in John 13:5-10:

> Then He poured water into a basin, and began to wash his disciples' feet and to wipe them with the towel with which He was girded. So He came to Simon Peter.

Peter was dumbfounded by this break of tradition. Jesus was not washing his own hands but the disciples' feet. Peter got it figured out mighty fast, and his surprise echoes through his response:

> He said to Him, "Lord, do you wash my feet?" Jesus answered and said to him, "What I do, you do not realize now, but you will understand hereafter." Peter said to Him, "Never shall you wash my feet!" Jesus answered him, "If I do not wash you, you have no part with Me." Simon Peter said to Him, "Lord, *then wash* not only my feet, but also my hands and my head." Jesus said to him, "He that has bathed needs only to wash his feet, but is completely clean; and you are clean, but not all *of you*."

Did you notice in those five verses that Jesus refers to two cleansings? He refers to the initial bath, the consecration cleansing. That is why He says Peter is clean. If someone has had a bath, he is completely clean. Then He refers to the daily cleansing, which is the foot washing. He who has bathed needs only to wash his feet. When you walk around in the world, you get your feet dirty, so you need your daily cleansing.

Ephesians 5:25-27 speaks of that initial or consecration cleansing. We also have another verse that deals with our daily cleansing from our walk in the world. We get ourselves dirty in a spiritual sense, and for this we need a daily cleansing. It is found in 1 John 1:9 and is sometimes called the believer's wash rag. As we confess our sins to the Lord, we need to remember 1 John 1:9:

> If we confess our sins, He is faithful and righteous to forgive us our sins and to cleanse us from all unrighteousness.

We need to turn to Him whenever we realize we have sinned and confess those sins to Him. He then takes the believer's wash rag and faithfully and righteously washes our sins away and forgives us. We need those daily cleansings as well.

16. ANOINTING OIL AND INCENSE

ANOINTING OIL DESCRIPTION

Exodus 30:22-33 describes the anointing oil. Verses 22-25 read:

> Moreover, the LORD spoke to Moses, saying, "Take also for
> yourself the finest of spices: of flowing myrrh five hundred
> *shekels*, and of fragrant cinnamon half as much, two
> hundred and fifty, and of fragrant cane two hundred and
> fifty, and of cassia five hundred, according to the shekel of
> the sanctuary, and of olive oil a hin. You shall make of these
> a holy anointing oil, a perfume mixture, the work of a
> perfumer; it shall be a holy anointing oil."

Back in Exodus 25:6 it was mentioned that spices were to be
gathered for the purpose of making anointing oil and incense, so at
this point in our study, the spices are to be used for the anointing oil.
They are described in detail. The New American Standard Bible
(NASB) and the New International Version (NIV) both translate the
phrase in verse 23 as "fine spices" or "the finest of spices." This is
fully consistent with the idea of quality that has pervaded all of the
instructions about the Tabernacle from the beginning. Everything
used for the Tabernacle was to be the best available, a worthy
offering to the King of the universe.

What is being described in verses 22-25? Myrrh came from the sap of
the balsam bush. Cinnamon is made from the bark of the cinnamon
tree. Cane is the pink-colored pit from the root of a reed plant. Cassia
is the dried flowers of the cinnamon tree. So these ingredients were
mixed into the olive oil to give it fragrance. This oil was described as

the work of a perfumer. Great skill was required to obtain the best compound of these ingredients. When the finest ingredients were handed over to experts, it was again consistent with the idea of skill and quality that pervaded every aspect of the Tabernacle.

Now how was the anointing oil used? We are told in Exodus 30:26-28:

> With it you shall anoint the tent of meeting and the ark of the testimony, and the table and all its utensils, and the lampstand and its utensils, and the altar of incense, and the altar of burnt offering and all its utensils, and the laver and its stand.

So the oil was used to anoint the Tabernacle and all its furniture; and as we shall see, Aaron and his sons were to be anointed with this oil as well. Now the purpose for the anointing is brought out in verses 29 and 30 of Exodus 30:

> You shall also consecrate them, that they may be most holy; whatever touches them shall be holy. You shall anoint Aaron and his sons, and consecrate them, that they may minister as priests to Me.

The act of anointing consecrated the Tabernacle, its furniture, and the priests. Again, consecration means to set something aside for special use. As we have seen before, whatever touches the consecrated things became consecrated itself. That which is unclean does not pollute that which is consecrated. Rather, the consecrated thing now sets aside the unclean item and makes it consecrated as well.

In Exodus 30:31-33 we come to the warning associated with the oil:

> You shall speak to the sons of Israel, saying, "This shall be a holy anointing oil to Me throughout your generations. It shall not be poured on anyone's body, nor shall you make any like it in the same proportions; it is holy, *and* it shall be

> holy to you. Whoever shall mix any like it or whoever puts
> any of it on a layman shall be cut off from his people."

This oil was to be unique in both its makeup and its use. To merchandise it, to sell it, to duplicate it without proper authorization, meant that the offender would be removed from the congregation either by banishment or by execution.

In verse 31 the rabbis took the phrase *for the generations to come* (NIV) or *throughout your generations* (NASB) to be a Messianic phrase. From it they inferred that the oil would be miraculously preserved and used in the Messianic Kingdom.[9]

Historical Significance

Historically, the oil was a symbol of the Holy Spirit, and the spices were luxury items, speaking of riches and the best that life could offer. The Tabernacle and the Priest were set aside for God's use through the agency of the Holy Spirit. The very best that Israel could offer was set aside through the agency of the Holy Spirit.

Messianic Significance

The oil symbolizes the fact that Jesus was anointed by the Holy Spirit. Jesus was anointed, not with the symbol, but with the reality that the symbol proclaimed. Jesus' anointing is prophesied in Isaiah 61:1, "The Lord God has anointed me."

---

[9] Dr. A. Cohen, ed., *The Soncino Chumash* (Soncino Books of the Bible), (Soncino Press: Brooklyn, NY), page 543.

The fulfillment is found in Luke 4:16-21 where we learn:

> And He came to Nazareth, where He had been brought up; and as was His custom, He entered the synagogue on the Sabbath, and stood up to read. And the book of the prophet Isaiah was handed to Him. And He opened the book and found the place where it is written, "The Spirit of the LORD is upon Me, because He anointed Me to preach the Gospel to the poor. He has sent Me to proclaim release to the captives, and recovery of sight to the blind, to set free those who are oppressed, to proclaim the favorable year of the LORD." And He closed the book, gave it back to the attendant and sat down; and the eyes of all in the synagogue were fixed on Him. And He began to say to them, "Today this Scripture has been fulfilled in your hearing."

Jesus was set aside and anointed with the Holy Spirit to do His mission. Acts 10:38 tells us:

> *You know of* Jesus of Nazareth, how God anointed Him with the Holy Spirit and with power, and *how* He went about doing good, and healing all who were oppressed by the devil, for God was with Him.

Other cross-references concerning Jesus' anointing are Matthew 3:16-17; Mark 1:9-11; Luke 3:21-22 and John 1:32-34. These passages also speak of the anointing that Jesus received.

Application

Let's consider this thought. Every believer is set aside for God's use by the anointing of the Holy Spirit. This is why you and I are referred to in scripture as saints. The word *saints* simply means holy ones or set apart ones. All believers are holy, and in position (because of the gracious treatment we have from God), we are set apart for God. John 14:16-17 says:

> I will ask the Father, and He will give you another Helper, that He may be with you forever; *that is* the Spirit of truth, whom the world cannot receive, because it does not see Him or know Him, *but* you know Him because He abides with you and will be in you.

You are set apart because the Holy Spirit indwells you.

First John 2:27 tells us:

> As for you, the anointing which you received from Him abides in you, and you have no need for anyone to teach you; but as His anointing teaches you about all things, and is true and is not a lie, and just as it has taught you, you abide in Him.

Not only does the Holy Spirit indwell us, but He also teaches us personally.

Ephesians 4:30 says:

> Do not grieve the Holy Spirit of God, by whom you were sealed for the day of redemption.

Because you are set aside by the Holy Spirit, because you are indwelt by the Holy Spirit, and because you are sealed by the Holy Spirit, you can be sure that you are eternally justified. Since the Spirit of God indwells you, you cannot lose your justification. If you are in any doubt about your eternal security, please review the verses above. They should assure you of your position before God.

INCENSE DESCRIPTION

Moses describes the incense used in the Temple in Exodus 30:34-36:

> Then the LORD said to Moses, "Take for yourself spices, stacte and onycha and galbanum, spices with pure frankincense; there shall be an equal part of each. With it you shall make incense, a perfume, the work of a perfumer, salted, pure, *and* holy. You shall beat some of it very fine, and put part of it before the testimony in the tent of meeting where I will meet with you; it shall be most holy to you."

Earlier in Exodus 30:1-10, we studied the Altar of Incense itself, and now the actual incense to be used on that altar is described.

The item called *stacte* in the NASB (or *gum resin* in the NIV) is a powder made from the hardened drops of the myrrh bush. It was very, very rare and incredibly valuable. Onycha is made from the shell of a variety of clam or some kind of a shellfish that is found in the Red Sea. Galbanum was a rubbery resin of thick, milky juice from the roots of a shrub that thrives in Syria and Persia. Frankincense is the resin from the bark of a plant that grows in southern Arabia. It is also extremely rare and extremely valuable. Southern Arabia had a monopoly on frankincense.

Just like with the anointing oil, special skill was demanded for compounding this incense. Therefore, someone skilled in the manufacturing of perfume was needed to mix the incense. It was to be made expertly, rather than in a sloppy or low quality manner.

Salt was added to the mixture and was ground up very fine for use on the Altar of Incense. Why salt? There are a number of opinions although nobody seems to really know what contribution it would make. Some think that salt was added to insure rapid burning; others think that it was added to create a white smoke. Still others think it was a preservative. Believe it or not, some think the use of salt added to the fragrance. So those are four opinions as to why salt was added to the mixture.

A warning similar to that associated with the anointing oil accompanies the description of the incense in Exodus 30:37-38:

> The incense which you shall make, you shall not make in the same proportions for yourselves; it shall be holy to you for the LORD. Whoever shall make *any* like it, to use as perfume, shall be cut off from his people.

The incense was to be unique and to be considered most sacred. Failure to properly consider it in that manner would result in being ejected from the assembly of Israel. This comment may mean either banishment or execution.

Historical Significance

Historically, we discover that incense is a symbol of fervent and contrite prayer.

Messianic Significance

The Altar of Incense symbolized Jesus as a man of prayer. The incense that was used upon the altar would symbolize the actual prayers uttered by Jesus. The High Priestly Prayer found in John 17 is an example of one of His prayers.

Application

We should also be characterized as people of prayer. Our lives should be like fragrant incense before the LORD. The emphasis on the Altar of Incense and the incense itself points out to us how important prayer is in God's point of view. This should not be regarded as a kind of repetitive, unnecessary section of the study, but as an emphasis. The emphasis on the need to pray, to have a personal relationship with God and talk with him throughout the day, deepens our relationship with Him. Paul tells us in 2 Corinthians 2:14-16:

> But thanks be to God, who always leads us in triumph in Christ, and manifests through us the sweet aroma of the knowledge of Him in every place. For we are a fragrance of Christ to God among those who are being saved and among those who are perishing; to the one an aroma from death to death, to the other an aroma from life to life. And who is adequate for these things?

That is the way our lives should be. Notice that our lives are not necessarily going to be easy. If we are that aroma, the sweet fragrance of Christ among people who are perishing, they are not going to be too happy with us. We will be reminding them of their sin and their separation from God and the fact that they will be judged by God. So from death to death is a very graphic description of the way we appear, the way our aroma is to those who are not going to be saved, to the ones who are perishing. But to those who are being saved, then our life will be an aroma from life to life; it will be a sweet smell, something a person enjoys.

I dwell on this because that is what happened to me. I got involved in a college group when I was a young man, about 19 years old, and this Christian college group had something that I had never ever experienced before. The people had a deep and genuine love for each other, and they had a personal relationship with God. I was fascinated by all that, but I could not quite put it all together. I did not know what it was, but I was attracted to these people, and I wanted what they had.

After I became a believer, I came across this section in 2 Corinthians. I suddenly learned what had happened. When I was among the people participating in that group on campus, I was smelling the aroma of life unto life. Those kids just exuded this wonderful presence that I wanted as part of my life. I could not quite put my finger on it, but it was just so great, so attractive, and is not that the way a fragrance is? It is a sweet smell; it just attracts you. You enjoy the aroma; you enjoy being around it. That is the way I was with those people, and that is the way our lives should be so that people will be confronted with their choice. Are they going to give their lives over to God and trust Jesus as their Messiah, or are they going to turn their backs on Him? "And who is adequate for these things," Paul says. This is a great responsibility, to live our lives before the world as a fragrance. But remember, that fragrance evokes two reactions, two responses.

That brings us to a final thought for application in our study on the Tabernacle. We have finished Chapter 30 in the book of Exodus. We have taken a look at all the furniture, all the items of the Tabernacle, how it was constructed, and finally we close with the incense that was to be put on the Altar of Incense.

Our final application is a very important one. We have to realize that we are a temple of the living God today.

The Tabernacle that we have spent several chapters studying was a temporary dwelling place for God. It was a shadow of spiritual truth, an audiovisual lesson that God used to teach us about the Messiah and about Himself. In contrast, if you have received Jesus as your personal Savior and Messiah, then you are His permanent dwelling place. As such, you are now God's temple. 1 Corinthians 6:19 says:

> Or do you not know that your body is a temple of the Holy Spirit who is in you, whom you have from God, and that you are not your own?

Since we are temples to the living God in a very dark world, we ought to shine out as lights in this world. Ephesians 5:8-9 tells us:

> For you were formerly darkness, but now you are Light in the Lord; walk as children of Light (for the fruit of the Light *consists* in all goodness and righteousness and truth.)

That is the way we ought to live our lives in the world because we are no longer part of the world; we are no longer part of that darkness. Our lives now need to be characterized by goodness and righteousness and truth. That is the type of life that God's temple should reflect. That is the type of person we should be.

CONCLUSION

What have we learned in these chapters? In Exodus 25-30 we took a look at the Tabernacle. We considered its construction and the materials used to build it. We also looked at the historical and Messianic significance of the building.

The Tabernacle had much to teach us about Jesus, about *Yeshua*. He was a man of prayer. He was a mighty King. He loves us and provided atonement for us. He is the One who did away with the separation between God and man. He is the One who offered Himself as a substitute in our place. He is the One who cleanses us and the One who goes into the presence of God and who brings us into God's presence. He is the One who is the Light of the World. He is the One who sustains us and the One who prays for us. He is our High Priest. He personally bears our sins.

And Yeshua (Jesus) is even more than all of this. He is the second person of the triune God. As such, He is the God of Abraham, Isaac, and Jacob who dwells between the *cherubim*. This is the One we worship, the Son of God, Jesus the Messiah, our Savior and our Lord.

Amen.